ADVANCE PRAISE

"The real war on women is the left telling them what to think, what to wear, and what to do. *What Women* Really *Want* is a passionate plea against feminism written by three courageous and determined ladies who are on the front lines fighting for freedom, faith, and family."

—GLENN BECK, #1 BESTSELLING AUTHOR AND FOUNDER OF THEBLAZE.COM

"This is a must-read for anyone who loves freedom, and wants to pass on that legacy of freedom to their children." —SEAN HANNITY

There are a lot of fun things that can be said about a title like this, but I think these authors are really onto something here. This is what we all should want— especially the mothers of the best generation. It is going to impact jobs, family, and the future of our children. —FRED THOMPSON

"Morgan, Gina and Ann-Marie are heroically combating the phony "war on women" by explaining in brilliant and no uncertain terms what women really want—and it has nothing to do with money and fast cars."

—DR. JAMIE GLAZOV, EDITOR *FRONTPAGE* MAGAZINE AND AUTHOR OF *UNITED IN HATE: THE LEFT'S ROMANCE WITH TYRANNY AND TERROR*

"Ann Marie, Morgan, and Dr. Gina are modern day women of Sparta, possessing the impeccable strength, honor, and conviction to stand valiantly in defense of this Country. In *What Women* Really *Want* these conservative heroines articulate the real "War on Women", the lies of progressive socialists. The Constitutional Republic known as America will survive as long as courageous women guard her dignity and character. Ann Marie, Morgan, and Dr. Gina are such women, their book is a must read, a needed prescription, and I graciously stand with them."
—ALLEN B. WEST, LIEUTENANT COLONEL (US ARMY, RETIRED), MEMBER OF THE 112TH US CONGRESS AND AUTHOR OF *GUARDIAN OF THE REPUBLIC: AN AMERICAN RONIN'S JOURNEY TO FAITH, FAMILY AND FREEDOM*

"What do women really want? These three powerful conservative women cut through the lies and distortions of leftist feminism to remind us of some important truths about women, men, families, and society. *What Women* Really *Want* is a refreshing, entertaining antidote to the cant and hypocrisy of the contemporary feminist movement, which (as this book shows in so many ways) is in reality profoundly anti-woman. Murrell, Brittany and Loudon deserve the gratitude of every woman and man who wants to see a restoration of sanity in American society." —PAMELA GELLER, HUMAN RIGHTS ACTIVIST AND AUTHOR OF *STOP THE ISLAMIZATION OF AMERICA*

"What man doesn't want to know what women (really) want? And who better to tell us than Morgan Brittany, Gina Loudon, and Ann-Marie Murrell? This book is an extraordinary challenge to the dreary feminist dogma that poisons relationships and ruins lives. A must-read for any woman and any man who is trying to find a way out of the swampland of selfishness, resentment, rage, and victimhood posturing that the Left has led American culture into over the last few decades." —ROBERT SPENCER, *NEW YORK TIMES* BESTSELLING AUTHOR OF *THE POLITICALLY INCORRECT GUIDE TO ISLAM (AND THE CRUSADES)* AND *THE TRUTH ABOUT MUHAMMAD*

"What men really want are women who really want what women really want."
—EVAN SAYET, AUTHOR OF THE KINDERGARDEN OF *EDEN: HOW THE MODERN LIBERAL THINKS AND WHY HE'S CONVINCED THAT IGNORANCE IS BLISS*

"Three beautiful, female, feminine powerhouses! Wow! A strong woman can live her values of God, country, home, family, have her career and still be a man's woman. What a message for girls and women of all ages. And a great book for men who believe that militant feminism has co-opted womanhood. Not so fast. *What Women* Really *Want* will become the bible to lead women to get off and stay off the feminist plantation and learn what a fulfilled life really is. Murrell, Brittany and Loudon have done it and written it. Kudos!" —BASIL HOFFMAN, ACTOR

"The PolitiChicks swizzle a little testosterone and estrogen, then spit truth in the face of the modern day news machine. I promise you, if you read *What Women* Really *Want*, you will find rectitude, possibly vicissitude, but never, never Obamadude!" —DWIGHT SCHULTZ, ACTOR

"This is one of the most relevant books written about American male-female relationships in years. I first met the Politichicks at CPAC, we became fast friends, and we have conducted numerous interviews over the years. Besides being gorgeous, intelligent, and worldly, they are very grounded people. This book is a guide for the modern relationship's quest of life, liberty, and the pursuit of happiness, the American Dream. Thank God for the Politichicks and the common sense they bring to the new Americana."
—CHARLES BUTLER, HOST OF *THE CHARLES BUTLER SHOW*

"When I think of Patriots, of individuals who have shown they are fearless in the face of tyranny and unyielding in their defense of Liberty and Justice, three California women--Ann-Marie Murrell, Dr. Gina Loudon and actress Morgan Brittany --are at the top of that list." —TIM DONNELLY, CALIFORNIA ASSEMBLYMAN AND 2014 CALIFORNIA GUBERNATORIAL CANDIDATE

"There is no such thing as the cookie cutter woman in today's society as the demands of women both professionally and personally are increasing. Who better then Ann-Marie, Morgan, and Gina to help explain this new role and the importance of the conservative female then three women who themselves have broken free of the limitations and stereotypes placed on them by the liberal left."

—SCOTTIE NELL HUGHES, NEWS DIRECTOR FOR *THE TEA PARTY NEWS NETWORK* AND AUTHOR OR *ROAR: THE NEW CONSERVATIVE WOMAN SPEAKS OUT*

"What do women really want? Nobody knows better than these three strong, wise, beautiful articulate warrior women! From global issues to personal ones, from family matters to national ones, co-authors Murrell, Brittany and Loudon approach this wide array of topics with grace, eloquence and passion, and, naturally, a woman's perspective. If you've been wanting to know how YOU can make a difference but haven't yet found inspirational role models that resonate with you, this is the book for you. This is the book that will provide the understanding of today's issues, the guidance through the distortions that have got us here, and the roadmap to find our way back. For activists and culture warriors of any gender, this is the book you need."

—KAREN SIEGEMUND, FOUNDER OF *RAGE AGAINST THE MEDIA*

"For years Dr. Gina, Ann-Marie, and Morgan have been fighting on the front lines for conservative values. *What Women Really Want* helps you understand why they continue their fight and also serves as a firm reminder of why we should never take our freedom for granted."

—DAVE BRAY, LEAD VOCALIST *MADISON RISING*

"These fierce and fearless women are tireless defenders of freedom and liberty . . . and they do it with style." —MIKE OPELKA, EDITOR-AT-LARGE *FIREWIRE* NEWSLETTER

"These women have been on my popular radio show because they know so much, including what women really want, and their new book will surely not disappoint you." —MARK ISLER, HOST OF *THE MARK ISLER SHOW*

"In an age where women have been hit from all sides by so-called experts with life-lessons on whom, why, how, and what they should want in life, *What Women Really Want* is a book from real women who actually have answers. This book does not contain mere musings from helpless and whining Hollywood hysterics. It contains information that can help women cut through to the truly important, while it also throws a lifeline to men who are willing to admit they do not have all the answers to what women want. If you are looking for tips for fame and fortune from celebrities who are among life's most unhappy, this is not the book for you. If, on the other hand, you are looking for clarity from clear-eyed, grounded, gifted women of wisdom, you've found your book."

—CONGRESSMAN LOUIE GOHMERT

"The War on Women is really a war on today's Renaissance woman who doesn't want to be enslaved, patronized, or labeled. I recommend *What Women Really Want* by the original PolitiChicks Murrell, Brittany, and Loudon for all courageous women across America who want to be warriors without emasculating men and without compromising their convictions. It explains the bad and the ugly of party politics, sheds light on the victories and pitfalls, and inspires today's woman to fight against the cultural forces trying to destroy our spirit, our families and our country." —SHARRON ANGLE, PRESIDENT NATIONAL FEDERATION OF REPUBLICAN ASSEMBLIES, CHAIR OF *OURVOICEPAC* AND 2010 SENATORIAL CANDIDATE AGAINST HARRY REID.

"*What Women* Really *Want* represent the beginning of a new era of feminism where women derive their strength by respecting true femininity and not by being locked in the 60s radical anti-male, anti-family, anti-God and anti-life movement." —NONIE DARWISH, FOUNDER OF *ARABS FOR ISRAEL* AND AUTHOR *THE DEVIL WE DON'T KNOW: THE DARK SIDE OF REVOLUTIONS IN THE MIDDLE EAST*

"Some sisterhoods are formed through blood. Others are formed through fire, passion, and love. That's Ann-Marie, Gina and Morgan. Honored to belong to such a sisterhood."—SONNIE JOHNSON, TEA PARTY ACTIVIST, POLITICAL COMMENTATOR, AND FOUNDER OF *DIDSHESAYTHAT.COM*

"Fighting the cultural lies imposed on young women, and implanted by the liberal media, the PolitiChicks are advancing conservatism through their sharp and unconventional message of hope."

—CALEB BONHAM, EDITOR-IN-CHIEF OF *CAMPUSREFORM.ORG*

"Captivating, inspirational, and embodying the patriotic tradition of Rosie the Riveter, three women break ranks with the sisterhood to reveal the true essence of the female. In an era where traditional femininity is under sustained attack from cultural elites, *What Women* Really *Want* in its call for a female sea change is not only brave, refreshing and irresistible, but critical to the American future. It will have you burning from the soles of your feet for America."

—NICK ADAMS, AUTHOR OF *THE AMERICAN BOOMERANG*

"This book rocks! And it is long overdue. For decades "womanhood" has been a political football for the Leftist agenda, and Ann-Marie, Morgan, and Gina have sounded a resounding clarion call for all women to wake up and use their brains to achieve real empowerment. Women, heed this call to take a stand for the truly liberated woman. Go Politichicks!" —GARY GRAHAM, ACTOR

"Rather than a mythical 'war on women,' these three women are field generals in a new 'war by women.' It is a war being fought door to door by a resurgent class of conservative female activists, thought-leaders, and ideological renegades willing to sacrifice for a better tomorrow. Read this book if you are looking for a training manual to join the fight." —DAN BONGINO, CANDIDATE FOR MARYLAND'S 6TH CONGRESSIONAL DISTRICT AND AUTHOR OF *LIFE INSIDE THE BUBBLE*

"Dr. Gina, Ann Marie, and Morgan understand that the strong, savvy woman isn't influenced by whimsy like what is spouted on TV. They know that their equality comes in the rights guaranteed by the US Constitution, and they understand freedom today and how to keep it. Men and women who want to keep their liberties need to read *What Women* Really *Want* so that they know the path to restoration in this republic. I recommend the truth in this book!"

—STEVE BANNON, EXECUTIVE CHAIRMAN, *BREITBART NEWS NETWORK*

"What woman really want! You couldn't have three better suited to explain it. All three ladies are attractive, intelligent, strong—mothers, wives, and friends. Loudon, Murrell, and Brittany lay it out and explain what conservative woman need to do to take back this society and this country. Great Job Ladies!"

—JOE MESSINA, HOST OF *THE REAL SIDE*

"In my twenty years of political activism, the one truism that stands time and again is that women are the heart and soul of this movement. *What Women Really Want is* a testament to that soul, and is a must-read for women gathering the courage to fight to defend liberty--for them, for their families, for all Americans." —ANDREW LANGER, PRESIDENT OF *THE INSTITUTE FOR LIBERTY*

"These successful women have found that the secret to good fortune comes from being engaged, motivated and free to pursue their dreams. It is a rejection of the current popular narrative that women can only survive with a big, over-powering government that caters to their every need. They all have the inspirational stories that can enhance your life." —SAL RUSSO, COFOUNDER OF *TEA PARTY EXPRESS*

"Isn't it terrific when beautiful women do beautiful things? Dr. Gina Loudon, Morgan Brittany, and Ann-Marie Murrell's book *What Women* Really *Want* explores everything from politics to popular culture to psychology and beautifully illustrates how smart, savvy conservative women can help turn the tide in today's not-so-perfect America." —LELA GILBERT, AUTHOR OF *SATURDAY PEOPLE, SUNDAY PEOPLE: ISRAEL THROUGH THE EYES OF A CHRISTIAN SOJOURNER*

"Dr. Gina, Ann-Marie, and Morgan nail it. Great life lessons, they have that rare ability to understand that femininity and strength can coexist. They demonstrate that we should celebrate the differences between men and women and that it is time we bring an end to the beta male epidemic." —CHUCK WOOLERY

"Morgan, Gina and Ann Marie are *not* just three pretty faces . . . well, maybe Gina is. Okay, she's totally going to punch me in the shoulder for that. In all seriousness, all three of them are smart, original thinkers, and conservatives need to read what they have to say about women's issues."

—JOHN HAWKINS, *RIGHT WING MEDIA*

"The spirit of Abigail Adams lives and breathes in these pages. This book stokes the fires of redemption for women everywhere—women who desperately want a restored femininity and feminism, but whose hope and tenacity are dampened by today's toxic political landscape. These stunning and insightful women stake their claim as modern day Shadrach, Meshach, and Abednegos, refusing to bow to modern culture's allowances and idolatry. Follow their banner."

—DR. DATHAN PATERNO, CLINICAL PSYCHOLOGIST, AUTHOR OF *DESPERATELY SEEKING PARENTS* AND *LADIES AND GENTLEMEN*

"I wholeheartedly endorse *What Women* Really *Want*. Women are better than men at getting the job done. I disagree with every other word in this book!"

—TAMARA N. HOLDER, FOX NEWS LEGAL AND POLITICAL CONTRIBUTOR

"It appears what women really want is an overweight guy with a fine mind. Who knew? And who knew that really wasn't and isn't what this incredible book is about. (Pity). It's about a call to arms and common sense. Take it from these beauties; they see the beast. Do you? Read . . . and learn . . . before it's too late."

—NEIL CAVUTO, ANCHOR AND SENIOR VICE PRESIDENT, FOX NEWS CHANNEL AND FOX BUSINESS NETWORK

"I have waited for a book to come along that exposes the lies, and this one nails it! As a warrior on the front lines with these three women, I am so happy that other women will have the chance to learn the stories and strategies in this book!"

—JENNY BETH MARTIN, *TEA PARTY PATRIOTS*, COFOUNDER AND AUTHOR OF *TEA PARTY PATRIOTS THE SECOND AMERICAN REVOLUTION*

"This book is *exactly* what freedom-loving women need. Dr. Gina, Morgan, and Ann-Marie speak truth to liberal feminist power. Their weapons in the fight to take back America: facts, faith, humor, and good old-fashioned common sense. You go, gals!" —MICHELLE MALKIN, AUTHOR, BLOGGER, AND MOM OF TWO

"Republican 'war on women?' What a joke! Women are quite literally the backbone of the conservative movement in the US. Where would conservatism be without Sarah Palin, Michelle Bachmann, Ann Coulter, Phyllis Schlafly, Heather Higgins, Katie Pavlich, Monica Crowley, Gina Gentry Loudon, Amy Kremer, Jenny Beth Martin, and so many others? Exactly nowhere!"
—DR. RICHARD AMERLING, PRESIDENT OF *THE ASSOCIATION OF AMERICAN PHYSICIANS AND SURGEONS*

"Feminism permeates messaging to young women from culture to college classrooms. *What Women* Really *Want*, gives us permission to lead influential and world-changing lives without requiring us to buy into the lies associated with the feminist agenda." —AUDREA TAYLOR, PRESIDENT & COFOUNDER, *IM2MORO*

"While we may not often agree with the means and methods required to solve our nation's problems, I can certainly agree that these are three women of considerable intelligence who are as well informed as they are well intentioned. Now that Murrell, Brittany and Loudon have chosen to shine a light on what women *really* want, we of the weaker sex—I refer, of course, to men—stand to be considerably better for it." —RICK UNGAR, SENIOR POLITICAL CONTRIBUTOR AT *FORBES* AND ON-AIR LIBERAL ANALYST ON FOX NEWS & FOX BUSINESS

"*What Women* Really *Want* empowers women, proves class always trumps crass, reminds us to keep our priorities in check, and shows the world what a tour de force women can be when we work together."
—CATHERINE ENGELBRECHT, *TRUE THE VOTE* FOUNDER

"For far too long women have been following the lead and advice of other liberal women. Women are still not feeling fulfilled as they follow this path of trying to satisfy themselves with the prize of being empowered. It's a self-serving prize that ends up being as attractive yet unfulfilling as a mirage. However, I don't see Murrell, Loudon, and Brittany in that scene. I see glowing successful women with supportive husbands, and as wives who love making their husbands happy. They're living what a lot of women claim to want but can't have because they've been mislead about what a real woman is. Murrell, Loudon, and Brittany are blessed wives and mothers, and happy successful women. Why not grab some insight from them?" —ALFONZO RACHEL, SOCIAL / POLITICAL HUMORIST

"Ann-Marie, Gina and Morgan have done the impossible: they have written a book on feminism that men will enjoy. They realize that feminism is a celebration of women and not a war on men. *What Women* Really *Want* stands as a great work to show where modern feminism went off the rails and offers an alternative—that women can be strong and feminine without tearing down others, especially men.

"Gloria Steinem, Naomi Wolf and Betty Freidan watch out! There are new Sheriffs in town. . . . Oh! And it doesn't hurt that they're sexy too!"
—ARI DAVID, SOCIAL MEDIA EXPERT AND HOST OF *THE ARI DAVID SHOW PODCAST*

"Dr. Gina, Ann-Marie, and Morgan are three beautiful and brilliant women. If they're willing to tell men what women *really* want, I think it's in man's best interest to pay attention. I know I sure as heck will!"
—RUSTY HUMPHRIES, *THE WASHINGTON TIMES*

"With beauty and brains, Ann-Marie Murrell, Morgan Brittany, and Dr. Gina Loudon give voice to millions of women the Left doesn't want you to know exist. Ladies and gents, you gotta get this book."
—KATIE PAVLICH, AUTHOR OF *FAST AND FURIOUS: BARACK OBAMA'S BLOODIEST SCANDAL AND ITS SHAMELESS COVER-UP*

WHAT WOMEN REALLY WANT

WHAT WOMEN REALLY WANT

ANN-MARIE MURRELL

MORGAN BRITTANY

DR. GINA LOUDON

 WND Books

WHAT WOMEN *REALLY* WANT

Unless otherwise noted, Scripture quotations are from the Holy Bible,
King James Version (public domain).

Published by WND Books˚, Washington, D.C. WND Books is a registered trademark of WorldNetDaily.com, Inc. ("WND")

Book designed by Mark Karis. Cover photography by Marc Royce.

Graph on page 99 from *The Righteous Mind: Why Good People Are Divided by Politics and Religion* by Jonathan Haidt, copyright © 2012 by Jonathan Haidt. Used by permission of Pantheon Books, an imprint of the Knopf Doubleday Publishing Group, a division of Random House LLC. All rights reserved.

WND Books are distributed to the trade by:
Midpoint Trade Books, 27 West 20th Street, Suite 1102, New York, New York 10011

WND Books are available at special discounts for bulk purchases. WND Books, Inc.,
also publishes books in electronic formats. For more information call (541) 474-1776 or visit www.wndbooks.com.

Hardcover ISBN: 978-1-938067-14-3   eBook ISBN: 978-1-938067-15-0

Library of Congress Cataloging-in-Publication Data

Loudon, Gina, 1962-
  What women really want / Dr. Gina Loudon, Morgan Brittany, and Ann-Marie Murrell.
    pages cm
  Includes bibliographical references and index.
  ISBN 978-1-938067-14-3 (hardcover)
1. Women--Political activity--United States. 2. Women--United States--Social conditions. 3. Women conservatives--United States. 4. Christian conservatism--United States. 5. Right and left (Political science)--United States. 6. Republican Party (U.S. : 1854-) I. Brittany, Morgan, 1951- II. Murrell, Ann-Marie, 1968- III. Title.
  HQ1236.5.U6.L68 2014
  320.0820973--dc23

                          2014014246

Printed in the United States of America

14 15 16 17 18 19 MPV 9 8 7 6 5 4 3 2 1

Dedicated to the men and women in our lives who have helped make us who we are.
They know who they are.

CONTENTS

Acknowledgments   *xxi*

Introduction: "R"   *xxix*

PART 1: WHAT WOMEN NEVER WANTED   1

1. When the Lights Came On   3
2. A Conservative in Hostile Territory   27
3. The Psychology of Labels and Transformation   39

PART 2: WHAT MAKES A WOMAN   49

4. Hollywood and the Transformation of Our Culture   51
5. Issues That *Really* Matter to Women, and Why   65
6. Swapping Sanity: Loving the Unlovable   81

PART 3: WHAT WOMEN *REALLY* WANT   103

7. Creating an Army of Women from Scratch   105

8. Platforms and Stilettos   121

9. To Win Back Hollywood   137

10. Diligence and Tenacity: Staying the Course   149

11. Spartan Warrior Women!   165

12. Twenty Years from Today   175

Appendix A: The Declaration of Independence   192

Appendix B: The Bill of Rights   198

Appendix C: The Gettysburg Address   202

Appendix D: 12 Rules for Radicals by Saul Alinksy   204

Appendix E: The Politics of Lying by Bill Federer   207

Notes   210

Index   216

ACKNOWLEDGMENTS

ANN-MARIE MURRELL

First, to my almost saintly, wonderful, patient, funny, and very handsome husband, Mark Murrell, you are the main source of my strength, and I realize I'm the main source that zaps most of yours. I love you and appreciate you more than you'll ever know. To my son, Jason, from the day you were born, I became a better person and am constantly trying to make the world a better place for you. I love and respect you beyond all reason. To my mom (and Texas PolitiChick), Lou Ellen Brown, and my father, Gene Brown, thank you for raising me with a rock-solid, unshakable foundation. To my writer-author-columnist crazy kook sister, Lisa Brown, who is my best friend in the entire world and the funniest human being in the history of the world (and who will be the next Erma Bombeck), you give me such inspiration. My nephew Zachary Zanardi reminds me that the word *impossible* isn't a word used in our family. The Bledsoes and the McConnells, have been continuously supportive of my political career. I am forever grateful to my dear "rabbi" and "twin sister" Beverly Zaslow; to Mimi who I adore; my little bro Jamie Glazov and his Glazov Gang; my awesome friends Tim and Rowena Donnelly and AlfonZo and Carrie Rachel; my inspiring Cali-Israeli friend Lela Gilbert; brilliant author Evan Sayet (who calls my husband The Obstacle despite their great friendship); my Rage Against the Media friends Karen Siegemund and Marc Langsam (thank you for all the photos, Marc!); Ari David for all things Twitter; Dwight Schultz, Nick Adams in Australia, Jim & Mary Reilly, Basil Hoffman, Chele Stanton for the Touchstone bling, Patty Smith. Thank you to my Freedom Fighter friends Louie Gohmert, Nonie Darwish, Robert Spencer, Frank Gaffney, Daniel Greenfield; you have taught me so much. To Mark Isler and his ultra-cool mother, Ruth, and the Dennis Prager team; a special thank you to Rick Amato and Sutton Porter for having such belief in my abilities; Tamara Colbert, one of my role models; Liberty Alliance; Luke and JoAnne Livingston; Toots Sweet for creating our PolitiChicks theme song. I'm indebted to Jim Cross with RedWhiteBlueNews.com for giving me my first writing job. I'm grateful to editors John Ransom, Mike Opelka, and Jenny Jones (formerly of Patriot Update and PolitiChicks) for allowing me the privilege to write for them. My heartfelt thanks to Jason Browning for going above and beyond for PolitiChicks (in addition to your Gina duties). Thank you everyone at WND Books, especially Joseph Farah and Geoffrey Stone, and to our literary agent Jim Hart. To my friends and family in Hughes Springs, Texas, thank you for keeping me grounded. And of course I'm so thankful for my wonderful, beautiful, intelligent, and world-saving PolitiChicks coanchors Morgan Brittany and Dr. Gina Loudon whom I love and adore more than they could possibly know.

Thanks to our PolitiChicks Uber-friends/fans—there are too

many to mention but an extra virtual hug for Robert Patrick, Tom Lehner, Gary Rumer, Skip Press, David Poindexter, DJ Ford, Tito Pineta, Pastor Jack Martin, Rob Hart, Michael Keller, Mitchell Lamm, Sean O'Reilly & the Fox Five Fan Page.

Last but not least, a very gratitude-filled thank-you to all our current PolitiChick National writers: Tina Drake, Lainie Sloane, Patti Terrell, Brenda Collins Morris, Abigail Adams, Barbara Cook, Michelle Moons, Lydia Goodman, Lisa Payne-Naeger, Sonya Sasser, Lou Ellen Brown, Jin Ah Jin, Michele Holt, Elizabeth Vale, Courtenay Turner, Liz Harrison, Lori Branham Bennett, Ruthie Thompson, Julia Gregory Seay, Carolyn Elkins, Leslie Deinhammer, Katie Abercrombie, Julie Klose, Sandra Coburn, Elisha Todd, Margie Mars, BurkaChick, Karin Piper, Dr. Jacqueline Lang, Candace Hardin, Maureen Mullins, Pamela Anne, Resa Kirkland, Macey France, Anita Gunn, Shannon Grady, Jenny Kefauver, Kristen Snow-White, Laura Rambeau Lee, Alyssa Krumm, Danielle Saul, Kathryn Porter, Latisha Grady and the hundreds of former PolitiChicks writers who have come and gone through the years.

MORGAN BRITTANY

I never realized that writing a book was such a tremendous undertaking. Even though this was a collaborative effort with my two incredible coauthors it gave me a greater respect for people who put pen to paper (or finger to keyboard!).

I have so many people that I would like to thank for helping me along the way in this effort. Mainly I would like to express my gratitude to Ann-Marie Murrell and Dr. Gina Loudon who are joining me on this journey. They are two of the most genuine, loving, generous, and, may I add, classy, ladies that I have ever had the pleasure to work with and call friends. I could never have done any of this without either one of you.

In addition, I thank Sean Hannity, who was the first to give me the opportunity to voice my conservative views to a national audience, and Gary Sinise, who had the vision to create FOA for like-minded thinkers in Hollywood.

Thanks to Jay Hoffman, Beverly Zaslow, Al Han, Michael Finch, and the always entertaining Evan Sayet! Jason Browning has gone above and beyond the call of duty organizing the impossible. Thank you, Mel Flynn and Mark Vafiades from Hollywood Congress of Republicans and Mark Isler (and his beautiful mother), for having me as a recurring radio guest on his show, and thanks to the incomparable Jamie Glazov for allowing me to join him as part of The Glazov Gang. Many thanks to Mike Opelka who has known me since the early days, and to my new friends Rick Amato and Sutton Porter from *The Rick Amato Show*.

I deeply appreciate the opportunity that John Ransom and Michael Shaus gave me to write columns for *Townhall Finance* and to Liberty Alliance for adding me as a PolitiChick. Thanks as well to everyone at WND Books for their hard work in publishing our book.

Thank you to my friend the Honorable Judge James Rogan who took my calls during the Clinton impeachment hearings. A huge thank you and shout out to Governor Sarah Palin who is on the front lines and voicing her support to all of us standing behind her.

I am especially grateful to my dear friend on the front lines, Larry Klayman. I am so glad that we met during the Judicial Watch years. I also cannot forget the incredible Andrew Breitbart who gave all of us the strength to make our voices heard. He was and is a force that will never be forgotten.

A special thank-you to my dear friend Chele Stanton who made all of us look so incredibly glamorous with her Touchstone Jewelry. And I particularly thank three dear friends who have always believed in me through good times and bad: Cynthia and Charles McDonald have always been there for me and patiently listen to me vent, and Laurie Atlas Seiden, who although she lives across the country from me, still has always been there for me.

Finally, I thank my wonderful husband, Jack Gill, who has been by my side for thirty-three years. He is the best support system I could have and has encouraged me to take risks in my life when I was afraid. I know that no matter what happens, he will always be there. To my children, Katie and Cody, whom I love more than life itself and each day make me so proud, I love you and thank you for your support.

One final thank-you goes out to my father-in-law, the late Major General Sloan (Sandy) R. Gill, USAF (Ret). Sandy inspired me with our talks on Sunday nights, and his encouragement, passion, and incredible service to this country has enabled me to find my voice. Rest assured Sandy, I and millions of Americans like me will continue to keep fighting for the freedom and glory of this incredible country that we all love.

DR. GINA LOUDON

To the single best person I have ever known, my sweet John, thank you for being the strong, steady, solid voice of reason and love in my life all the time. Thank you for your unmatched wisdom, your unmitigated patience, and forbearing love. Thank you for believing in me and always being my refuge in the storms of life. Thank you for the dream-come-true life we live, that you worked so hard to achieve, and for always giving me the wings I need to chase my dreams. Most of all, thank you for giving me our five precious babies that make every moment amazing. N&F, MSJM <3.

Lyda, Lily Love, Jack (Tade), Samuel Christian, and Booce-Booce "Bo" Loudon: You are my treasure. My greatest accomplishment, my greatest refinement, my greatest loves, my greatest pride, my greatest challenge, my greatest humility, and my greatest purpose. I live every day for your future, and I love you USAMBEA. I always will. God willing, you will have a free America to one day know the love that I knew the moment I looked in your eyes and knew I had to fight for you. You are my world, and the reason I live and breathe. Being your mama is the greatest honor of my lifetime.

Chupi (Producer Jason Browning): Thank you for teaching me that every day is the best day of my life! Thank you for pushing me, believing in me, challenging me, adventuring with me, fighting for me, being behind the scenes making it all come together, for picking up the pieces, making it all right, making it better. You made the phrase "everyone needs their own Jason" famous, and it is never lost on me how much you sacrifice—how big the work, how little the thanks, and how unbelievably competent, brilliant, and wonderful you are. MSH 15, or bust!

To my mom, your faith inspires me, your love emboldens me, and your strength in the face of challenges makes me feel invincible. Thanks to Dale for being your rock so that you can be mine. I love you, ONPN. To my dad, who taught me the most, even if it isn't what he meant to teach me. I know you will never read this, but I want to say it anyway. I am thankful to God for you in my life, and it is my prayer that you can know Him and feel how He has always loved you, used you so mightily, and forgiven you so greatly. I love you, Daddy.

To my sisters: 1) My Smexi, Michelle Huffman—Thank you for reminding me what is good when I lose sight of it all too often. Thank you for loving all my curves and edges and the constant reminders of your love. You are a present I can't wait to open each day! 2) Angela Delay—my Dancin' Queen and my tambourine! I have had more laughs and more fun with you than anyone alive; I am blessed to have you, and I love you. 3) To my sister who gave me the gift of life in my son Samuel and to all of those women out there who choose life—what women really do want: #AdoptionNotAbortion.

I thank my current and former editors, agents, partners, publishers, colleagues and stylists: Andrew Breitbart, who believed in me first and named me "Troublemaker." Michael Walsh, Nicole Challans, John Ransom, Ola Hawatmeh, Tamara Colbert, Phillip Dennis, Bob Unruh, Dr. Dathan Paterno, Neil Cavuto, Bev Zaslow, Chelsea Schilling, Joseph & EF Farah, Geoffrey Stone, Jim Hart, Garth Kant, Laura Scotti & Don Crawford, Shante Schwartz, Diana Flegal, Lee Davis, Michael Hart, Bob Dutko, Brandon & Jared Villorani, Ray Lucia, Jr., and the Lucia family.

I'm grateful to my fellow warriors who inspire me, push me, have my back, hold me accountable, laugh with me, and make the battle worthwhile: my pastor and solid faith rock Jim Garlow, my Big Bro and close friend DJ Ford, The Adamses, Vicki Ambrose, Jen AmericanGirl, Chris Babb, Frankie Baird, Caroline Batycki, Scott Beason, Belle OftheBall, Tom Bendure, Tim Boren, April Braswell, Santiago Cano, Candace Chambers, Jamey Clements, Morgan Cody, Victoria Coley, Bert Collins, Jeff Coulter, Linda Judson Creviston, Dark Horse on the Roof, Kira Davis, Martha Doiran, Tim and Rowena Donnelly, Wayne Dupree, Sarah Dykes, Cam Edwards, Michael Elmore, Feisty Floridian, Deanna Frankowski, Melanie Reed Freeman, Dr. Gary, Ali Claire Genis, Xander Gibb, Ryan Girdusky, Joe Dan Gorman, Katherine Elizabeth Grantham, Cameron Gray, Sarah Greek, Zan Green, Dr. Isaiah Hankel, Rob Hart, Kevin Huffman, Rusty Humphries, Dr. Jim, Farida Joaquin, Jim Jorgensen, Michael Keller, Jeff Klein, Kelly Komadoski, Andrew Langer, Steven Laboe, Mitchell Lamb, Marc Langsam, Terri LaPoint, Carole Levine, Mikey Lawrence, Tom Lehner, Trish Lester, Luke & Jo Anne Livingston, Angela Love, Steven Maikoski, Fingers Malloy, Isabel Matos, Marybeth Meek, Rabbi Chaim Mentz, Penny Nance,

James Nathaniel, SSgt. Robert Norton III, Dr. Gina McNelley, Joe Messina, Shane Mincer, Zel Mitzel, Michelle Moons, Mary Moran, Mark Murrell, Sly Ocana, Sean O'Reilly, Kim Paris, Skip Palmer, Robert Patrick, Gregg Phillips, Katrina Pierson, Tito Pineta, David Poindexter, Keely Prohaska, Serafin Quintanar, AlfonZo & Carrie Rachel, Jeff and Ann Reed, Dran Reese, Richie Rich, Brian Rightof-Center, Stacey CW Roberts, Jes Romero, Karin Rosarne, Lila Rose, Gary Rumer, Sal Russo, Paula Sanning, Rick Sarmiento, Wayne Sasser, Randy Schaffer, Thomas Schmitz, Suzanne Sharer, Lavon Doris Shockley, Chris Skates, Lainie & Shannon Sloane, Tom Sizemore, Brian Smith, Deno Smith, Deauna Stafford, David Stephens, Christopher Stewart, Cathy Ellis Stone, Brian Stumpe, Rick Suryk, Courtenay Turner, Cyndi Brinkerhoff Uhlenhoff, Jack Watts, Jackie Wellfonder, Ruth Weiss, David Weissman, CJ Wheeler, Scott Wilke, Tollie Williams, Woody & Donna Woodrum, Glyn Wright, Bev Zaslow, Lisa Zimmerman, Gene Smith of Hoover Tactical Firearms in Birmingham, Alabama, and whomever I have forgotten on this list—you know who you are, and I thank you. To Father of heroic Benghazi SEAL Ty Woods Charles Woods and all our military heroes, we will never forget!

To my enemies, because I have learned so much from you.

To my audience whom I have to thank for everything. To my friends in the Show-Me State who will always be deep in my heart, and my Sweet Home Alabama, that I love so much. #RollTide

To the two most amazing women in media that grace the planet today, and my partners, for whom I am eternally grateful, Ann-Marie Murrell and Morgan Brittany. You are what this world needs. Shine!

To God, because You are my All.

INTRODUCTION

"R"

by ANN-MARIE MURRELL

Once upon a time, a group of people created the most perfect product ever made. This product could literally change the world if people would simply put it to use. They called this product "R." They built a building around R, and they filled the building with wonderful, patriotic people who were trained to sell R. Instead of advertising or using a large sign, they attached a very small, very tasteful *R* onto the front of the building. When some of the younger R people questioned this, they were told, "Our product doesn't need anything big and flashy to sell it; it is, after all, the perfect product."

The problem with this marketing strategy, or lack thereof, was that across the street from R was their main competitor, known as "D."

The creators of D also had a building, but in front of theirs was a gigantic rotating *D*, lit up with thousands of shining neon lights. Inside their building, they employed young people of all nationalities speaking all languages, and throughout the years they developed new technology and new ways of getting their D message out into the world. They created things like Facebook and Twitter, and as soon as they got bored with those, they started creating even *newer* ways to get their message across.

In front of the D building, young sign spinners tossed signs high into the air to generate attention. Others called out to people as they passed by, "You don't even need to come inside—here's a *free cell phone* for you! All you have to do to thank us is give us a call just before election time—or better yet, we'll call *you* to remind you who to vote for!"

And when children walked past the D building on their way home from school, D employees would give them *free laptops*, telling them, "Be sure to tell your parents the Ds gave this to you, because unlike those evil Rs, who hate everyone, we *love* children and care about your education!"

One day a couple of savvy young college students wandered into the D building. These young men had actually read their Constitution and Bill of Rights and understood fully what the Ds were doing. When they asked, "Who's paying for these cell phones and laptops?" they were told, "You sound like those evil Rs across the street!"

So the savvy young college kids went across the street and learned the truth about the perfect product stored inside the R building. But sadly, they saw that instead of fighting back against the lies being told by the Ds, the Rs were trying to change their product, to make it into something the D customers might someday want to buy.

The young men said, "No—stop! You don't need to change your product. It's perfect, and we can help you get the word out to the people! We can help you design new technology and spread your message!"

One of the older, more established Rs said, "Aw . . . How cute! We love young people. We're going to put you right to work answering phone calls at our phone bank and putting stamps on our mailers."

The young men looked over at the dusty rotary telephones and the stacks of papers, shrugged their shoulders, and left the R building.

They went down the street and saw another building, with a red, white, and blue "TP" out front. A TP worker said, "We believe in the Constitution, lower taxes, smaller government, and a free market system!" So one of the young men shrugged and said, "I'm in."

The second young man went a little further down the road and saw another building, with a giant *L* out front. A few college kids said, "We believe in the Constitution, and we want to legalize pot and prostitution!" The second young man said, "Meh, I'm in!"

As both young men entered their respective TP and L buildings, they looked back at building R. A tumbleweed was rolling across the empty parking lot, and a cobweb had formed on the very small, very tasteful *R*. Both men felt sadness, knowing that no matter what these other new people said, the Rs once had the perfect product.

The end.

Labeling people is a way of defining people and things in groups like Democrats or Republicans. However through manipulating definitions labeling can be a way of controlling or enslaving people. The left is masterful at using labels and manipulating terms to demonize their opponents. Rather than hanging on to the liberal and conservative terms that so polarize the country, throughout the book we try to use more objective terms as statist to signify those who want a centralized and controlling state and progressive to signify those who want less objective moral constraints in people's lives.

PART 1

WHAT WOMEN
NEVER WANTED

1

WHEN THE LIGHTS CAME ON

by ANN-MARIE MURRELL

No man, when he hath lighted a candle, putteth it in a secret place, neither under a bushel, but on a candlestick, that they which come in may see the light.

—LUKE 11:33

Nope, I wasn't born this way.

Many of the people I grew up with in my hometown in East Texas were—and still are—Democrats. Of course, they were never the scary, progressive folks that are trying to destroy America today. They could more accurately be described as really nice JFK Democrats: good, decent, hardworking people with extremely high morals and values. I truly believe if some of them really knew what their party has turned into, they would flock to the Rs in droves. Most of them believe there are two types of Democrats: the California kooks and them. What they don't understand is that what is happening in LA and New York City and other cities is spreading fast, and if we don't fight it, even my little hometown won't stand a chance.

These days, all my friends know me as a very strong (and

somewhat opinionated) conservative. They know of my work with PolitiChicks, have seen my interviews, and have read my political articles—but the inconvenient truth is that I've been a Republican only since September 11, 2001. It took a major tragedy to get me where I am now, but I believe my life as a former Democrat gives me an insight that not all conservatives have. (At least that's what I tell myself to keep from sinking into a guilt-induced depression.)

I first became aware of politics the summer of 1974, when my parents forced my sister and me to watch Richard Nixon resign his presidency. We couldn't understand why anyone would want to watch such a sad-looking old man on TV when it was a perfectly sunny day outside; but we obediently watched until we were given the go-ahead to get back to our bike riding.

In high school, I decided the Democratic Party was for me for one reason: a cute boy.

Cute Boy's (CB) father was running for Texas state representative, and I figured that campaigning for him would mean I'd get to spend more time with CB. It was a wonderful summer, and I had a ton of fun working on that campaign. Of course, to this day I have no idea what CB's father actually stood for or what type of state rep he ended up being. But as a Democrat, I never really used my brain too much when it came to politics. I simply didn't care. If the candidate I was voting for seemed like a nice person who cared about the world, that's all that really mattered.

Soon after, my political brain left my body, and at age fourteen, I became enamored with Jimmy Carter. It happened on our way to Disney World when my family and I took a side trip to Plains, Georgia. We stopped at the Carter family gas station, and that is where I met my very first celebrity—the president's infamous brother, Billy. I posed for pictures with him, Billy in the middle, grinning broadly with his arm around me while balancing his Billy

Beer (and a cigarette) in his hand. Because of that strange encounter, and reasons unbeknownst to me now, four years later I couldn't wait to use my brand-new voting privilege to help get Billy's brother elected to a second term.

I fought as hard as a fun-loving college freshman could fight for President Carter's reelection. I did things I now consider blasphemous: replacing Reagan–Bush signs with Carter–Mondale ones and debating anyone who said anything bad about President Carter. I would argue that Carter was a "beautiful, peace-loving man" who had only the best interests in the United States. I didn't care what people said about the silly economy or the gas lines; none of those things really mattered to me at the time, and I was devastated when he lost.

Later, when I was a struggling and still politically ignorant young actress living in Los Angeles, I continued voting for all things Democrat, as did everyone else in my life at the time. I once even participated in an antiwar/antinuclear protest (which I later found out was led by ultraradical Jerry Rubin). To be totally honest, the real reason I went to that protest wasn't as much about the cause as it was the clothes. My actor friends and I thought it would be fun to dress like hippies, in peace necklaces and paisley items from Melrose thrift shops, and hold protest signs. We mostly giggled and acted like idiots; I'm sure even Rubin was happy when we left early.

Back then, the only time I remember talking politics with my artist friends was during Screen Actors Guild elections; and even then, someone else probably had to explain what we were supposed to vote for. The word *self-absorbed* comes to mind.

(Seriously, writing this, I don't even like myself right now. Bear with me, conservatives; it all has a happy ending.)

My final political blunder came via Bill Clinton. It was the 1990s. I was now married to my husband, Mark, who had always been a strong Republican—so we had to work very hard to completely avoid political discussions during the Clinton years. When we did talk politics, it usually ended with me saying something like, "I just believe in him, that's why!" and leaving the room. Despite all the bad press I had read about Bill Clinton's personal life before the election, I believed he was my new Jimmy Carter, and ironically, I was also convinced Clinton was everything President Reagan and President George H. W. Bush were not. Bill was young, charismatic, and seemed to be in touch with the people. He had the same type of dynamic personality that I imagined someone like John F. Kennedy would have had (not to mention the same type of bad-boy reputation to which, before I met Mark, I had always been personally drawn). So I happily voted for Bill Clinton. Twice.

Throughout Clinton's presidency, basically everyone—including his supporters—knew what a scumbag husband he was, so few were surprised when the Monica Lewinsky stories came out. We had already heard about other women who'd allegedly had affairs with the president, but they all eventually "went away." I think we all thought Lewinsky would "go away" too, but she didn't. Somehow I was able to put my personal moral values aside (and turned a blind eye to his lack thereof), and I decided Bill Clinton's sexual problems were between him and his wife and not the entire world.

But then he lied.

As soon as Bill Clinton—"my" president—looked everyone in America straight in the eyes and said, "I did not have sexual relations with that woman," the love affair was officially over for me. *Allegedly* cheating on his wife was one thing, but getting caught red-handed in the Oval Office and continuously lying about it until DNA evidence backed him into a corner was unconscionable. I was happy he got impeached and disgusted when he didn't step down. Unlike Nixon, that would have been a resignation I *would* have wanted to watch on television.

While the sex scandals were playing out, I closely watched his vice president's reaction to everything. I waited for Al Gore to step up—to separate himself from Bill Clinton. I don't know what I wanted him to do or say. I just wanted him to do *something*. He did nothing.

So the question was, why? I was a young woman with considerable intelligence and a very strong work ethic, so what was it about the Democratic Party that continually seemed so appealing to me? The answer was the same for me then as it is today for all the blind progressive supporters, and it basically comes down to one word: *propaganda*. Really great propaganda. Somehow the mainstream media have been able to convey to people that Republicans are rich and elitist while the Democrats are for the people. If I had thought about it at the time, I would have realized that all of the hip, progressive actors in Hollywood probably had much more money than most of the Republican "elitist" politicians I had vilified. And, ironically, the people who continually denigrated those "rich elitists" were themselves rich elites, like Walter Cronkite, Dan Rather, and Peter Jennings. Yet the Democrats simply *seemed* to be more about the people. I was in my twenties and had to work several jobs just to stay alive, and, bottom line, I completely bought into the premise that Republicans were rich, old people who had no clue what it was like to be a young, struggling American.

As a young Democrat, I listened as the media told me that America was a bully, and that all war was unnecessary. In the '70s, all I ever heard on the news was how pointless Vietnam had been. Then in college, I looked on as the media called President Reagan a warmonger and told Americans there was no reason to continue building our "war arsenals." They insinuated that if only the big, bad tyrants of the United States would stop building weapons, maybe there would be peace on earth.

For whatever reasons, I bought it.

The first time I didn't vote blindly for the "D" was in the 2000 elections, after becoming thoroughly disenchanted with Bill Clinton. I remember standing in the voting booth that year, still unsure which candidate should get my vote for president. My mother, a retired Texas teacher, had been an avid fan of former governor George W. Bush; she told me he had been a big supporter of education in Texas, and she had nothing but great things to say about him. But being a prisoner of the mainstream media, all I was hearing about Bush were his past issues with drugs and alcohol, and after Clinton, I didn't want to discount potentially damaging personal problems ever again.

In a panic, I did what I believe many Americans did that year: I voted for Ralph Nader. The media made a huge deal about the election being rigged, and about hanging chads; they couldn't imagine how someone like Ralph Nader could get so many votes. They claimed George W. stole the entire election—but I understood why he won. I believe many Democrats did what I did that year and threw away their votes in disgust. After the election, I didn't think it mattered *who* was president.

But all that changed on September 11, 2001, when airplanes flew into the World Trade Center's twin towers and the Pentagon. I watched, as did the entire world, as America turned into something completely different than it had been the day before. And as I watched, everything I had previously believed—about almost everything in life—began transforming.

My first thought—the one that caused my "let there be peace on earth" dreams to crumble—was that this was not a fair fight. How could we possibly battle a type of evil that would crash innocent people into *nonmilitary* buildings?

When I saw the towers crumbling, I felt the same type of

helplessness I'd experienced as a child when my father died. I was also reminded of the fear and panic I felt just after the Northridge earthquake of 1994. Holding my then-six-year-old son close to me, I wondered, *What's next?* We were safe inside our building, but without access to radio or TV we had no idea what had happened to the rest of Los Angeles. Did my sister and her family survive? Were our friends okay? Was there going to be another, more devastating aftershock? Watching the towers in New York collapse, I felt the same terror in not knowing what was going to happen to America. I was afraid—until I saw newly elected President George W. Bush standing in the midst of the rubble, his arm around a fireman, telling us we were going to survive. He said this would never happen to our country again—and I believed him.

I knew in that instant why a man like Al Gore could never have been my president after September 11, 2001. We needed a man with backbone; a man who would unabashedly stand up for us in a fatherlike way; a man who could not only reassure Americans that we would be protected and safe, but who would also send a definitive, unequivocal message to the rest of the world—whoever and wherever our enemies were—that attacking the United States would *never* be okay. No matter what character defects the media told me he had, I knew that George W. Bush was a president who would die trying to protect the United States of America. And despite the mistakes he may have made during his presidency, that much I still believe to be true.

Before 9/11, I didn't understand why America needed arsenals of weapons for some imaginary enemy out in the world. For most of my life, I had considered myself a free spirit who believed in peace and love. On September 10, 2001, I didn't understand what evil really was—but I fully understood it the following day.

I became a Republican on September 12, 2001. I called my local GOP office, literally with tears streaming, and told them I couldn't be a Democrat anymore. That little "gap" in my brain—the thing that separated unicorn and rainbow wishes from logic and reality—was suddenly bridged, and everything finally made sense to me.

From there, it was like a domino effect. While reexamining my life, I found myself having a series of epiphanies: "If I was wrong about that, I was wrong about that, too . . . and that . . . and that . . ."

Bottom line: *There are enemies out there who hate us and want us to die.* They plot against us in sneaky, terrifying ways never imagined by our Founders or any of the brave soldiers who fought in American wars.

I guess it takes some people longer to see the light than others; it certainly did for me. But the thing about the light is that once you've seen it, you're a fool if you ignore it or try to pretend it away. I'll never be that person again.

The next step I took in my political life wasn't quite as dramatic as the first—but realizing what I needed to do required a type of courage I never thought I had.

BIRTH OF A POLITICAL ACTIVIST

In 2008 I was still a noncommittal, passive conservative. Of course I saw things I didn't like or agree with politically—including a swelling tide of support for a little-known senator from Chicago. I was working part-time as a children's director at a church, and I read and researched as much as I could about then senator Barack Hussein Obama. On the surface he sounded wonderful—a young, energetic man who was building excitement and enthusiasm everywhere he went. The fact that America could finally have a black president was absolutely thrilling to everyone—myself included. Most of all, a lot of my Democratic friends who didn't like Hillary Clinton were ecstatic to have such a viable alternative. But wow! Talk about red flags! Rumors were flying all over the place about everything from Obama's birthplace to his communist ties to his religion. Beyond all of that, the thing that most shocked me about my Christian friends who were blindly supporting Obama was the fact that he supported partial birth abortion. Even if they supported "regular" abortion, the fact that they were excusing the indisputable butchery of partial birth abortion was stunning to me.[1]

Throughout 2007, with the impassioned buildup leading to the 2008 elections, I sometimes envied my political activist friends who continuously posted news and updates on Facebook. Back then I had approximately five hundred Facebook friends, who, politically, were split almost exactly down the middle—two hundred–something conservatives from Texas, and two hundred–something statists from Southern California. I kept my posts completely apolitical, consisting of either prayer requests for friends or benign updates like, "Picked a lemon from my lemon tree and made chicken piccata for dinner. Yum!"

Meanwhile, I became a voracious reader and researcher of all things political. My mother, Lou Ellen, was my English teacher throughout high school, and she instilled in me a deep love and respect for books. So I read everything—civics and history books, presidential biographies, and every political pundit book I could find. I read Ayn Rand's *Atlas Shrugged* twice, back to back.

Then I discovered Mark Levin.

I was on vacation and brought along Levin's *Liberty and Tyranny*. That book opened my eyes to so many things I had never considered or even known before. I was so excited that I did something my mother considers blasphemous: I wrote notes all throughout the margins. I read and reread that book, and continue rereading it every chance I get.

(Side note: A few years ago, I got to meet Mark Levin at a Reagan Library event. I already felt like a groupie, so I brought along my copy of *Liberty and Tyranny* to show him how much I appreciated him. He seemed to get a kick out of it and somehow found enough blank space to autograph my book for me.)

In addition to reading and researching, I watched Fox News, thanks to my parents, and Glenn Beck as often as possible. Despite all the news and information packing my brain, publicly I remained safe and cozy in my nonpolitical cocoon.

That is, until news came out about a case that, for me, was far too important not to speak out against.

In a nutshell, two men were standing near the front door of a polling place, dressed in military-like garb and threatening and intimidating voters as they walked by. One of the men was holding a nightstick, aka a weapon. In another era, the two men could have been white supremacists associated with the Ku Klux Klan; in this instance, they were members of the New Black Panther Party. Without valid reason or cause, Attorney General Eric Holder suddenly dropped the 2008 New Black Panther Party voter intimidation case.

I was *furious*. Bartle Bull, a *Democratic* activist, called the case the most serious act of voter intimidation he had witnessed in his career.[2] The evidence had been overwhelming, including a video of club-wielding Panthers standing outside a polling place in Philadelphia, threatening people as they entered.

Holder's dropping of the case led to very reasonable allegations that the Department of Justice was setting a precedent of "looking the other way" in regard to cases involving minorities—and these accusations made Holder mad.

"Think about that," Holder said in a House Appropriations subcommittee meeting. "When you compare what people endured in the South in the 60s to try to get the right to vote for African Americans, and to compare what people were subjected to there to what happened in Philadelphia—which was inappropriate . . . to describe it in those terms I think does a great disservice to people who put their lives on the line . . . *for my people.*"[3]

"*My people*" was the headline screaming from every conservative media outlet in America—and instead of President Obama intervening and trying to pull Americans together, he did nothing.

Holder's early actions led many conservatives to believe that instead of being the "uniting president" Barack Obama had promised he would be in campaign speeches, he and his administration almost immediately instigated an "us versus them" mentality in every aspect of life in America. On a personal level, the activist deep inside of me began bubbling to the surface, fighting to get out, reminding me of the loss and regret I experienced when I was five years old.

My father, Jerry Bledsoe, was my hero. He was a preacher, teacher, and performer. He performed in almost every play and musical at the El Paso community theater. I was almost always with him, sitting on the edge of the stage, watching him sing "The Impossible Dream" or play Mr. MacAfee in *Bye Bye Birdie*.

On November 21 my sister and I were planning to go with our father to a school function, but at the last minute my sister got sick, and neither of us was allowed to go. I was furious. I wasn't sick, so I didn't understand why I had to stay home too. I threw a major tantrum—the kicking and screaming and crying kind. Before he walked out the door, I made damn sure my father knew just how angry I was at him, and yes, I told him I hated him.

On November 22 my mother woke me up very early that morning to tell me my father had been killed in a car wreck. In that instant, I experienced intimately what death meant, the finality of it all. And from that day on, I vowed to never let anyone or anything go without a fight.

Flash forward to 2008. A presidential administration was actively working to "transform" my country, and when I realized what was happening and how far they planned to go, the little dormant activist inside of me started shouting, "*Do* something! Don't let her go without a fight! Don't live with one more regret that you didn't do or say everything you could possibly have done and said to save your country!"

Very soon after Holder's "my people" statement, I began writing. I posted, ranted, and raved on Facebook—carefully separating my California progressive friends from my Southern, Republican friends. Then one of my Facebook friends, Jim Cross, the editor of *Red White Blue News*, asked me if I would write for his blog. The only writing I had ever done was in high school, when I was the editor of our school paper, *Hoofbeats*. Other than that, I'd never had anything published.

Of course, writing about politics would be *very* different from writing about football games and homecoming dances. I had also witnessed the wrath (and sometimes threats) that many of my political friends received. It was one thing to rant on Facebook to my two hundred–something conservative friends, but was I ready to share my political beliefs with the rest of the Internet? Was I prepared to put myself on the line? Another aspect was that it could potentially involve my family being ostracized too. Were *they* ready for that? I took several days to pray about it, and after getting the overwhelmingly supportive blessings of my family, I very reluctantly told Jim I would write for him.

And that was that. I had no idea how many words were inside of me, and I sometimes found myself writing from sunup to sundown. I loved the research, loved learning, and especially loved feeling that I was doing something more than simply being a bystander while my country was being trampled.

After a while, I stopped separating my Facebook friends and just let it all hang out. The fallout came almost immediately. I lost practically all of my two hundred–something progressive friends right away, but then something amazing happened. Soon after coming out of the conservative "closet," my Facebook numbers started growing. Fast. Within about a year, I went from having around two hundred friends to the maximum of five thousand. And once Facebook allowed non-friends to follow your page, I opened my page to the public and am currently at more than forty-two thousand (and growing).

While writing for *Red White Blue News*, I covered a Michael Reagan event at the Reagan Library. Apparently Michael read my article and asked me to write for his site, Reagan Reports for America (ReaganReports.com). (By the way, years later I finally garnered the courage to personally apologize to Michael for campaigning against his father when I was eighteen; he forgave me and told me I wasn't the first to do so.)

Eventually, I ended up writing for a dozen or so conservative websites, including Patriot Update, which eventually birthed PolitiChicks (but that's another chapter). What I soon realized was that I had finally found my true calling in life. It was, of course, the last "calling" I ever would have imagined for myself, and truthfully, on a list of ten thousand callings, I'm certain I never would have chosen this particular one. But here I am, many years later, a political activist.

The main reason for all this passion and commitment is because after my father's tragic death, I learned that no matter how seemingly infallible something may be—no matter how strong, how secure, or how much you love it—it can all be gone in an instant. If we could take a time machine back to ancient Rome and tell them their great empire would eventually fall and that tourists would someday visit the ruins of their monuments and the Colosseum, they would laugh in our faces and call us conspiracy theorists.

Like Rome, America is a strong republic; but also like Rome, America is not infallible. The problems we've been experiencing here in America didn't arise overnight, and they certainly did not begin with Barack Obama.

It took decades to get to the point in history where two thugs could intimidate and threaten voters with billy clubs without being punished. And what's worse is that after decades of skewed thinking, we are at a point where if you questioned the problem of the thugs getting off scot-free, you were called a racist.

It took decades to get to the point where innocent Americans— old and young—found themselves standing in airports with their arms in the air, like criminals, in a backscatter X-ray device being publicly (albeit virtually) strip-searched. The reason is because the politically correct didn't want to hurt the feelings of the *real* potential terrorist who might be standing behind you—and if you questioned this, you were called "religiously intolerant."

And it took decades to get to the point where a small group of people who believe in nothing told all of us who do believe in something to take down our crosses and dismantle our Nativity scenes because it insulted their eyesight. And when we questioned that, we were called "ignorant" and "backward" and "unenlightened."

The good news is that the other side is definitely starting to hear us. MSNBC, CNN, and all the other non–Fox News networks are literally falling apart before our very eyes. They are imploding because Americans have finally figured out that the mainstream news is (and has, for the most part, always been) the most one-sided, biased, and unfair organization since the Gestapo. Old-school journalists, the type that "go along to get along" and do whatever their statist bosses tell them to do, are officially considered despicable to most conservatives and will never be blindly trusted again. The alphabet networks are now thought of in the same way people think of the *National*

Enquirer—there's maybe a thread of truth in what they tell you, but the rest of the story is either hidden or completely made up. (We're watching you, mainstream media, and we're mad.)

Because of my father's death, I learned as a child how fleeting time and life can be. I also learned to pray, but with an understanding that although God doesn't always give us what we want, He will provide us with what we need. And He wants us to do good works in response to His provision. Soon after November 22, I memorized the following poem that I found in a Jolly Rancher candy box. I have used these words throughout my life:

> Sitting still and wishing,
> Makes no person great.
> The Good Lord sends the fishing,
> But you must dig the bait.
> *(Author Unknown)*

BREAKING UP WITH THE MAINSTREAM MEDIA

Dear Mainstream Media—MSM for short,
> We need to talk.

> We've been together as far back as I can remember. As a child, I fell in love with the Beatles watching you!

> I remember when you changed from black-and-white to color, and watching *Bewitched* and *The Partridge Family* and *The Brady Bunch*. But a person can only take so much abuse, and I know what you've been saying about me.

> You didn't even try to be subtle about it. You didn't talk about me behind my back; you did it right there in public, on TV and in movies, for the entire world to see! You and your actors called me names and ridiculed my beliefs. You have denigrated my religion, my politics, and every principle I stand for. And you did the same thing to all of my family and friends.

But Mainstream, it's also the lies you've been telling all of America—the cover-ups—the way you don't ever talk about things that are really important.

What about Fast and Furious? You barely ever mentioned it. And now you're not talking about Benghazi, the IRS attacking innocent citizens—do you just NOT CARE? Is all of this really just for a political agenda?

So, Mainstream, to make it real, to make it permanent, I have cut you out of my life completely. I no longer watch any network television, and my family and I will never support movies that involve the actors, producers, and directors who have shown us so much contempt and disrespect.

And I admit—it has not been easy without you. I miss watching my favorites, like *Survivor* and *Dancing with the Stars*—it's been a sacrifice—but Mainstream, the good times do not outweigh the bad, and I'm so glad my eyes are finally open.

The sad thing is, you need my friends and me a lot more than we've ever needed you, because without us, you would be nothing—nothing but a lot of dead, useless air.

So, thanks for the memories, Mainstream Media, but I'm moving on up. The tribe has spoken—and that's the way it is. Good-bye.

The catalyst for making me write this Dear John letter to the mainstream media is because of two supposed "family" sitcoms: ABC's *Modern Family* and NBC's *The Office*. Before jumping to the conclusion that I left because of the gay theme running throughout both shows, that was only part of the reason.

In *Modern Family*'s "Mistery Date," "lovable" Cameron[4] (played by Eric Stonestreet) was coaching his gay friend Dave (played by actor Matthew Broderick) on how to have an affair with a married man.[5] I suppose the only decent part of this scene was that Cameron asked Dave to make sure the wife and kids weren't home before seducing his date. Here is a transcript of the scene:[6]

DAVE: He's married. To a woman. Yeah, she's out of town. I don't know. They must have some sort of arrangement or something.

CAMERON: So what? If they know about it, who cares? You're not ready for a relationship anyway. Just have some fun.

DAVE: It feels weird. He has other people coming over. I think I'm gonna bail on this.

CAMERON: He's just feeling you out like you're feeling him out. I promise you, these other guests will mysteriously cancel.
(Dave gets a phone call, finds out other guests cancelled.)

DAVE: You were right. The other guys just cancelled.

CAMERON: See? Now listen to me. You're gonna have two margaritas. Maybe start a third. Laugh at his jokes. But not in that high falsetto thing. Something more manly. Let's practice.

DAVE: I'm not gonna laugh for you. You can be very controlling, you know that?

CAMERON: Why does everybody say I'm controlling?

DAVE : Gotta go.

On the same night, I watched an episode of *The Office*, entitled "The Target." Throughout the season, the big joke was that Oscar, a self-righteous gay man, was having an affair with uptight Angela's Republican state senator husband. Soon after having a baby, Angela learned about the affair and tried to hire a hit man to have Oscar killed.

Funny, no?

Yeah, not so much. From *The Office*:[7]

ANGELA: You are incorrigible! I just saved your life.

OSCAR: You're welcome! You hired someone to hit me with a pipe! You deserved every bit of it!

ANGELA: You made my husband gay.

OSCAR: What—what I did was wrong, and I have to live with that every day. But your husband is gay. He was gay when you married him!

ANGELA: No. No.

OSCAR: Angela, until you face that, you're gonna be confused and angry for all the wrong reasons. But if you want to blame me for the whole thing, go ahead—I won't stop you. Hit me. You have my blessing. Hit me.

ANGELA: Well, are you gonna let go of it? Because part of the blame is definitely on you.

OSCAR: Angela, it's a lead freaking pipe. God!

ANGELA: Aah! You were supposed to be my friend.

OSCAR: I'm so sorry.

At least he apologized.

Let's break it down. First of all, on *Modern Family* Cameron's character is supposed to be the fun-loving, teddy bear–like guy, the one who seems to genuinely care about his family and friends. He and his partner had already adopted a little girl and were in the process of adopting another. However, in "Mistery Date," Cameron is urging his gay friend to sleep with a married man—in the married man's house, no less, and surrounded by pictures of his children.

Cameron's only caution was to make sure no one's home—and he then encouraged Dave to get drunk and go for it.

Take out the entire gay element and this is still one of the lowest forms of debauchery and immorality humanly possible. Cameron is supposed to be a father to two little children; would he be okay if someone encouraged his partner to cheat like that? And yet this is a television series that is heavily advertised as a *family* show.

Then there's *The Office*. From the beginning season, Angela was written as the mean, uptight Republican, while Oscar, like Cameron, was the fun-loving, "caring" guy on the show. In season 9, episode 8 (and a few preceding it), the running joke was that Angela was too stupid to realize that her husband was not only gay, but was also sleeping with her office mate (and supposed friend), Oscar. The gist was that Angela *deserved* to be cheated on because she was so mean to people—and that Oscar *deserved* to be with someone he loved.

After watching this back-to-back garbage, I realized you shouldn't feel the need to take a shower after watching so-called family comedies on television.

In this day and age, does immorality matter? Does character count? You might say, "It's only a TV show; what does it matter?"

I contest that the answers are yes and yes, and it matters a great deal. One of the reasons we're where we are in this country is because we looked the other way too many times. We allowed too many small, subtle things—like these two sitcom episodes—to go on unquestioned. We lived up to our "silent majority" moniker, keeping quiet when we saw things we didn't like or disagreed with. Does "only a TV show" matter? Yes it absolutely does, especially when it is so blatantly and clearly mislabeled as something it is not. In unsupervised and impressionable hands—our youth—watching cute Cameron push another gay man to sleep with a married man is cancerous.

Unfortunately, after so many years—decades—allowing this to

go on, the entire world is in a bit of shock because we're all starting to speak up about it. They've gotten comfortable, being able to put forth their poison unchallenged. So that's a good thing.

As for me, the night I watched those two shows, I was so angry that my first instinct was to throw our television set off our balcony. Since I couldn't lift it, my next thought was to completely disconnect by calling my cable company and having all the network television removed from our home. My husband quickly nixed that idea. (I think his exact words were, "Hello, Super Bowl?") Plus, what good would it do to live inside a bubble and not even know what's happening out there in the mainstream world? So instead, I blocked all the network channels from our main television, and I now only watch network if/when it is work-related. During this time, I also turned my "Break Up" letter into a video for PolitiChicks.tv. It got a lot of traction in the conservative blogger world, and for a while I was a mini-champion to some of my friends for having turned my back on network television.

But my convictions came into question when in November 2013 I got a call from CBS's *Dr. Phil* show asking me to participate in an episode about racial profiling. I received the call just as Dr. Gina and I were literally sitting down to begin a panel at a conference. I immediately felt a combination of guilt and fear. Do I participate in a CBS show, an entity that I had personally deemed as the "enemy"? And would the not-necessarily-conservative Dr. Phil—Oprah Winfrey's buddy—chew me up and spit me out for the entire world to see?

Of course, I was extremely fortunate to be sitting next to someone who knows better than almost anyone in the conservative world what it's like to be put to the test on network television—Dr. Gina Loudon. As you'll read in one of her chapters, Gina and her family experienced the wrath of the mainstream media in a major way on ABC's *Wife Swap*, and Gina has also made several appearances on Jon Stewart's *The Daily Show*. Since I had Dr. Gina and a roomful of potential counselors right there in front of me, I put the question to them. Should I or shouldn't I do the *Dr. Phil* show? The reactions were mixed, varying from "Don't do it no matter what" to "Go for it!" Later, after posing the question to my social media friends, I received several well-intentioned private messages basically telling me I would be a fool to go on any type of network television and represent conservatism.

Ultimately, after praying about it, I did the show. My appearance wasn't nearly as dramatic as the Loudon family's on *Wife Swap*; if anything, it was kind of fun. My friend Ari David was also on the show, and although Ari's a stand-up comedian, he took the more dramatic route, while I went for funny. I got a few big laughs (the intentional kind), while Ari, well, did not.

Is it worth it—for the conservative cause—to risk potential ridicule and slanted editing, to appear on network television? And other than Fox News and talk radio, without having any network television on our side, will conservatives ever be able to effectively get the message across of "who we really are"?

In November 2013, Media Research Center's Dan Joseph conducted interviews on a college campus, asking kids to define the difference between "conservatives" and "progressives."[8] Their answers were almost identical to what I always heard growing up in the '60s—basically, that conservatives are rich, greedy, and closed minded, while progressives care about people, the environment, and social issues.

The common denominator between the misguided youth of yesterday and today was and is the media.

Like most children of the '60s, I spent many hours with my parents watching lovable, sweet ol' Walter Cronkite. Each night, he would end his news broadcast by saying, "And that's the way it is."

But *was* it?

Back then no one would have dared question Mr. Cronkite's journalistic integrity. However, he admitted in his later years that he was indeed a statist.[9] He also had some very strange, kind of creepy New World Order–like leanings.[10] Yet to this day I still hear conservatives talk about the "good old days" of Cronkite, Chet Huntley, and David Brinkley. "Those were real journalists," folks say, usually with a bit of sadness in their voice.

Perhaps the old-guard journalists were better than some of the scum buckets we have today, but in my opinion the sooner we discard the notion that anyone on earth can be completely "neutral" or "unbiased," the better off we'll be. Even the greatest journalists in the world have opinions about everything from which toothpaste they prefer to what they're going to eat for breakfast. People continually make choices and have preferences almost every moment of every day. So why would anyone believe that when it comes to something as important and impassioned as politics, suddenly—simply because someone is called a journalist—a person is unbiased? I contend that this is completely impossible, unless someone has been lobotomized or turned into a George Soros robot. (Okay, that one could actually be a possibility . . .)

The inconvenient truth is that in this very biased world, only one side of the story is being told: the progressive's side. They are defining who we are, because they control the all-powerful mainstream media. So what in the world are we supposed to do about it? Many of my conservative friends tell me they haven't watched network television or paid money to see a movie in years; yet when you look at the network ratings, it seems someone is certainly paying those advertising bills. Feature films may not be doing as well as they were before the economy got Obamanized, but studios aren't closing, and movie stars are continuing to rake in their millions. Many conservative bloggers—myself included—rant, rave, and complain about how horrible the MSM are, but other than these things, what else can we do?

Dr. Karen Siegemund, creator of a group called Rage Against the Media (www.rageagainstthemedia.org), said in an interview, "First, we hope to create a greater awareness of how duped we all are by the media. The journalists on whom we rely for our information are utterly unethical in their agenda-driven reporting, and sadly are exceedingly effective at crafting an entirely false 'reality' that too many simply believe.

"The extent to which the media is willing to lie to the people in order to protect the powerful is simply beyond comprehension," she added. "People need to be made aware of this, and [to understand] that the media does not have our best interest at heart."

Later in the interview, Siegemund said, "[Progressives] believe that all the ills we suffer are due to George Bush, that Republicans are in the way of progress, that Obama is the Messiah, that the Tea Party is a collection of racist haters, that whatever happened in Benghazi was unfortunate but that far worse happened under George Bush, . . . that Obamacare will cure all the flaws of a greedy insurance system and will provide us all with superior health care; that Joe Biden is an intellectual titan while Sarah Palin is an immoral ignoramus who incites violence; that government programs solve problems and private enterprise is the root of all evil; that, in short, Republicans are evil and Democrats are the saviors of the world."[11]

The good news is that we have come miles from where we were just a few short years ago, when people, including me, simply weren't aware of the media bias. I'm almost embarrassed to mention this, but if I don't, my parents will. When my stepfather had back surgery in 2007, I went home to Texas for a month to help out.

My parents live in an underground house deep in the piney woods of East Texas, and they have one television. Every day in '07 at 5:00 p.m., when Glenn Beck came on—no matter what they were doing—their world would stop. At first I was annoyed. I hadn't begun my political/reporting career yet, and I wasn't the news junkie I am now. I did my best to stay preoccupied; I cleaned closets, did yard work or whatever I could find to pass the time—but seriously, there's only so much you can do to pass time in an underground house . . . so eventually, I started watching Beck. And wow—that was it. Not only was I hooked, but when I got back home to California, my world stopped, too, at 5:00 p.m., when Glenn Beck came on. I'm not sure if he was the main catalyst for my political career (I blame Barack Obama for that), but he certainly made me aware of things I had never considered before. Beck also caused me to think outside the box—especially regarding the media—and reminded me to "do my own homework" when I had doubts.

All in all, my personal take on battling the media monster is to keep hitting it head-on. Being afraid of it is just silly—and ignoring it and wishing it away doesn't work. And as long as we do keep doing nothing, shows like *Modern Family* will continue encouraging Americans to think it's funny to cheat on spouses and sleep with married men. Gay or not.

2

A CONSERVATIVE IN HOSTILE TERRITORY

by MORGAN BRITTANY

Being powerful is like being a lady. If you have to tell people you are, you aren't.
—MARGARET THATCHER

I was born in California in the early 1950s. At that time California was the Golden State.

Many people were flocking there from all over the country because of the opportunities it offered. Due to the expanding defense industry, tens of thousands of people, including wartime and postwar migrants from across the nation, relocated to find jobs in the employment boom.

California not only lured people because of jobs, but the climate was considered perfect. It truly offered everything one could want.

Hollywood was booming as well, and there were growing opportunities because of the emergence of television. Previously, people would have to go to their local movie theater or stage production to see their favorite stars or musicians. Radio offered in-home entertainment, but it lacked the visual element that people demanded.

Television offered everything to a family, and it was now available in the comfort of your own home.

I was introduced to the world of television at the age of five, and not just as a spectator in my living room, but as an actual participant in front of the camera. My mother and grandmother had grand ideas for me and groomed me to be a little triple-threat star: actress, singer, and dancer. Off I went, to classes that taught me everything I needed to know, and sure enough, I was soon discovered by an agent.

At that young age I have little memory of what the political leanings of my family were. I only remember vague, fuzzy images of President Dwight Eisenhower on the tiny television set, and I knew that my mother was interested. I had no idea who he was and didn't hear much conversation at the dinner table about politics. I was more inclined to want to watch *Howdy Doody*. A few years later, though, I had my first encounter with the political leanings of Hollywood.

Back in 1960, child actors were sent on casting calls for television shows, films, and commercials. I remember distinctly one afternoon, going on one of these calls. It was an audition for Mobilgas. Funny how ads for gas companies, cigarettes, and the like were common-place up until the '80s, and then they just vanished from sight. The usual drill was to have all of the children line up, and the advertising executives from companies like McCann-Erickson or Foote, Cone & Belding would walk down the line and pick out the children they wanted to interview. I was one of the children picked to go to the next level. It was to be in a commercial where a family of four drives into a Mobil gas station, Dad tells the gas attendant to "fill 'er up," and at the end of the spot, the attendant gives one child a donkey and the other an elephant as a free giveaway for coming to Mobil. This was supposed to be a tie-in to the upcoming election in the fall.

When it got down to the last four children, they paired us up as brother and sister and asked us some questions. For those who remember, Art Linkletter had a program on TV called *Kids Say the Darndest Things*, and a lot of ad execs used that concept when interviewing children to see what funny things might be said. The first pair at this commercial audition were asked the question, "Who would you vote for, for president this year?" The little boy, who I remember was very precocious, answered loudly, "Richard Nixon!" The little girl stood there wide-eyed, not even understanding the question, and just nodded her head. I remember at that moment looking over at the casting director, and she looked at me and slowly shook her head from side to side. I was puzzled, but then the question came to me and my would-be brother.

"And who would you vote for, Kennedy or Nixon?" I had no clue what to say, but without hesitation, I took my cue from the casting director that the Nixon answer was wrong and firmly stated, "Kennedy!" A big smile came across the ad executive's face, and he nodded his head. Need I say more? I got the job. True story.

I didn't really encounter much political discussion over the next few years. I do remember that while I was filming an episode of *Lassie* in 1963, we were in the middle of a scene when an assistant director came in and said that President Kennedy had been shot. We ended up shutting down production for a few days, and I followed every moment of the story on television. I remember being riveted to everything I saw, from Walter Cronkite tearing up when he announced that the president had died, to the live, on-air killing of Lee Harvey Oswald by Jack Ruby. The whole nation mourned together, and there was no partisan divide. Everyone, no matter which party they belonged to, was in a state of shock that something like this could happen in our country.

By the time I turned sixteen, my childhood career was coming to a close. I entered high school, and really, for the first time, I attended classes like any other kid. Before that I had been in and out of school, mainly being educated on a studio lot. We were in the midst of the war in Vietnam, and my history classes were covering the war through news stories that dominated the press. It was a tumultuous time, and I remember how the kids were on two distinct sides of the war issue.

We had the antiwar protestors, who held demonstrations and sit-ins on campus, and then we had the boys who were pro-military and were preparing for their lottery numbers to be picked. You could not have found a more divided group of people in the mid to late '60s.

The hippie generation was in full swing. Drugs were readily available, free love was acceptable, and "the Man" was the enemy. The Establishment was something to be scorned, and the military was mocked and spat upon. I remember feeling lost and disconnected.

Here I was, barely sixteen, and I'd been in the workforce for more than eleven years! I had made money, supported my family, and grown up knowing responsibility and discipline. I was looking around at kids who had no concept of what the real world was like and had no idea what they were talking about. I was basically a thirty-year-old trapped in a sixteen-year-old's body. My friends were few because they could not identify with how I felt and what I had experienced.

My views were "old-school" to them, not "hip and with it." On one hand I desperately wanted to fit in, but on the other, I knew in my heart that my attitudes, morals, and work ethic were going to pay off in the long run.

By the time I was a junior in high school I was very involved in the civil rights movement. I had lived through the Watts Riots during the summer of 1965. The unrest hit close to home for me because I took tap-dancing lessons in Watts every Friday night from one of the legendary African-American dancers of all time. Willie Covan had been the dancing coach for Eleanor Powell during her MGM years. He and his wife were the most wonderful people I think I have ever had the honor of knowing, and I studied with him for years. When it became apparent that tensions were rising over the passage of Proposition 14 in California, which attempted to block the fair housing portion of the Civil Rights Act, Willie advised my mother not to bring me down there; it wasn't safe for a white person to be in Watts. I will never forget the pain in my heart the day I found out that my Fridays dancing with Willie would be ending. We all had tears in our eyes as we said good-bye, and it wasn't long after that that the Watts area ignited into chaos.

Because of my interest in civil rights, I was attracted to Robert Kennedy, who was running for president in 1968. I became a member of the Young Democrats of California and went on a massive get-out-the-vote campaign for the upcoming primary.

On June 5, 1968, our group was scheduled to attend the victory celebration for Kennedy's California primary win at the Ambassador Hotel. I had been fighting a bad respiratory infection for a few days and was not feeling my best. I wanted to be there, but at the last minute I decided not to go. Of course, we all know what happened that night, with the assassination of Senator Kennedy. I was devastated.

As I look back on the values of the Democratic Party in those days, they looked more and more like those of Republicans than of modern-day Democrats. The economic policies of John Kennedy, if spoken today, would mirror those of Republicans. Bobby Kennedy aggressively attacked corruption and targeted organized crime in a big way. He and his brother advanced the civil rights cause in a way that even Republicans came to respect. There were many progressive issues at the time, and many became instituted by the left, but Democrats back then weren't as actively progressive as they are today.

After high school, I wanted to attend college and become a journalist. I studied at California State University, Northridge, but

I couldn't afford to stay in school, so I decided to make a living doing what I knew best. I was offered a job as a dancer with Gene Kelly in Las Vegas. I took it, but only out of necessity. Over the years, I'd spent my income as a child actor supporting my family, and I was left with nothing. At eighteen, I knew I needed to grab the opportunity while it was still available.

In the early 1970s I left Hollywood and relocated to New York City. There, I changed my name, threw out my résumé, and started over. New York was a disaster in those days. The city was a crime-ridden, rat-infested sewer. It was on the verge of bankruptcy and politically was a corrupt mess. Most of my go-sees were in Times Square, and believe me: you took your life in your hands when you went to Broadway and Forty-Second Street back then. It was the boulevard of drug addicts, prostitution, and porn palaces. Not what you see today, with its Disneyland feel.

Muggings were everywhere, you couldn't walk through Central Park, and you didn't dare venture above 110th Street.

Democratic mayor "Abe" Beame presided over the city while I lived there, and I began to see the real effects of progressive policies and rampant corruption. The unions were in control of everything. They could shut down the city on a whim, and did. The NYPD was under investigation for widespread corruption, welfare spending skyrocketed, and the city was headed for default.

I was living in this chaos and watched it deteriorate in real time.

I got an offer to move to Japan during the '70s, and jumped at the opportunity. It was a great break for me to be the face of Kanebo cosmetics. I lived in Tokyo and traveled the world for two and a half years learning and discovering how America and Americans were perceived outside of our borders.

America was, in a word, *respected.* In the countries I visited before the Nixon debacle, we still had an untarnished glow that everyone in the world wanted to see. We were viewed as the land of opportunity, the road to success, and a place where you would not be afraid to speak and pray.

America represented freedom and liberty in a way that was magical to other nations. We were also respected for our military strength and our generosity to those in trouble in the world. I was one of the first American models to represent an Asian cosmetic company. We were so idolized by Japan and the Asian people that they wanted to do everything in their power to be like us. It was exhilarating for me, and I was so proud to be an American.

I returned home to the United States during the last months of Gerald Ford's presidency, and I settled back into my life in New York with an expanded view of the world. I had been out of the country for the Nixon–Watergate disaster and only followed it through the eyes of the rest of the world. I remember sitting in a café in Paris, reading the newspaper headline that proclaimed that Nixon had resigned the presidency. When the 1976 elections came around, I followed them closely.

I wanted Gerald Ford to be reelected, but I knew that with his pardon of Nixon, the odds were against him. No one really knew Jimmy Carter, but Americans were so tired of corruption and lying that they would have elected anyone who seemed new and untainted. Little did we know that all of America's hopes would turn into ashes.

Upon my return to New York, I continued a career in advertising. I had a comfortable income shooting commercials and doing magazine ads. Even though it was still difficult living in the city, with all of its crime and problems, I knew I had a better opportunity there than in Los Angeles. Ed Koch became the new mayor. At least he was more fiscally responsible than Beame, but heavy progressive policies still had a foothold, and the city was seeing little improvement.

Prices for everything were rising, and it became harder and harder for me to sustain an apartment in the city. I was very aware of the taxes being deducted from my checks, and I was becoming more conservative by the day.

In 1976 I was offered a role in an ABC pilot for a new series. *Delta County, U.S.A.* was the story of a small town in the South, and all of its scandals. It was being done in Hollywood, so I decided to move back there. A change in tone had come over Hollywood, and many of the new studio executives and investors were beginning to turn away from the gritty, earthy style of films to a more glamorous, glitzy type.

I suddenly fit back in, and television opened up to me. I shot the television pilot, but it didn't go anywhere. It was way ahead of its time because it was another attempt at a nighttime soap opera, and the networks weren't quite ready for it. *Peyton Place* had been a successful soap in the '60s, but nothing like it had been attempted since then. *Dallas* didn't come along until 1978, and it still took that show two years to catch fire. It wasn't until the "Who shot J.R.?" episode that the show became a hit.

In the late '70s, during the presidency of Jimmy Carter, I became more and more interested in the economy and monetary policy. Those years were filled with turmoil. We had double-digit inflation, high interest rates, oil shortages, and slow economic growth. I remember going to the store on Wednesday, buying extra groceries because I knew the prices would be higher on Friday.

There was general discontent among most Americans, surprisingly even in Hollywood. I was fortunate to be working steadily, and when that occurs, you grab the attention of top Hollywood agents and managers. A very powerful and influential manager with major television and film stars on his roster was interested in representing me and grooming me to be the next "big thing." We met one afternoon, and he laid out a plan and strategy for my future. I was a bit hesitant about his grandiose promises, but I let him talk. He did not know my background as a child actor and felt that I would be dazzled by all of his power. After all, what young actress wouldn't want to be represented by such a "mover and shaker"? At the end of the meeting, I thanked him and said that I would consider his offer. He came over to me then, and looked at my necklace. I was wearing my crucifix, as I always do, and he held it in his fingers. "If you work with me, you will have to lose this." I was stunned. "What?" I asked. "You can't show your religious views in Hollywood; you'll never work." I didn't know what to say at that moment, but after I got home, I made up my mind.

I placed a call to his office, thanked him for his time, and told him we weren't on the same page when it came to values and priorities. Later, after I had become one of the stars of *Dallas* and other films, I ran into this agent, and he knew that I had succeeded without hiding my faith.

With the '80s and the election of Ronald Reagan, I began to see and pay more attention to all politics. I started listening to conservative hosts, like George Putnam in California. What he said made sense to me. I learned about foreign affairs and wanted to educate myself on issues in case I needed to answer difficult questions in interviews. (Some journalists like to catch performers off guard. They love to ask about foreign relations or economic issues to blindside you. It only happened to me once, after that I was prepared.)

About a year into the Reagan presidency, I noticed that there was a tremendous dislike and disdain for our president. Sitting in the makeup trailer, I would hear vicious attacks against his administration, and jokes being made, and I never heard one word in rebuttal. It became obvious to me that the crewmembers and actors who remained silent and out of the conversation did not agree with the vocal members.

I was working on a series at Warner Bros. when one of the main actors went off on a rant against Reagan. I was standing off camera and must have rolled my eyes, because later, one of the gaffers approached me and whispered, "Are you a Republican?" I was afraid to admit it, but I nodded my head. "Me too!" He continued to tell me that most of the crew thought the way I did but didn't dare make it known for fear of being fired.

I realized that silence was the only option I had if I wanted to keep my job. Many times I had to grit my teeth in the transportation van on the way to location, listening to the misinformation that was being spewed. I wished I could have set those progressives straight on the facts, but didn't dare. It always amazed me that they had no qualms about making their opinions known; they just assumed everyone thought the way they did. To them there was no doubt that *everyone* in Hollywood was a progressive. Even the young actors, who were perhaps on the fence politically, followed in step and laughed and joked with the them. They wanted to be part of the majority no matter what.

Thankfully, no one ever asked me about my political views. I always just kept my head down and read a book or seemed uninterested. I never let my political beliefs interfere with my work.

Even though I would sit with my fellow actors and listen to their vitriol in the makeup room, I could put it aside, walk onto the set, and not let it cloud my performance. It doesn't seem to work that way with some progressives. Once they know you are Republican or conservative, they can't get past it. In their eyes you are a racist, homophobic, greedy person who doesn't care about anyone else. Some progressive producers and directors don't want to hire you because they can't stand the thought of hiring someone so despicable. The great director and playwright David Mamet has brilliantly chronicled this in his 2011 book *The Secret Knowledge*. Ask any conservative in

Hollywood and he or she will have similar stories.

I had remained silent for years and years—until I had finally had enough.

After 2001 I decided to speak out on behalf of conservative values and policies. I made a conscious effort to let people know my feelings, and I gave speeches to groups who would never have believed someone in Hollywood could be—*gasp!*—conservative. I raised money for candidates, spoke at events, and went to little towns across America just to motivate and show people that not all of Hollywood was crazy and out of touch. I reached out to Sean Hannity when he was putting together his first American concert and offered my help. Along with Gary Sinise and some wonderful country stars, like Lee Greenwood, we stood up with Sean to show support for America. Sean had me on his show as part of the Great American Panel on numerous occasions, and it became obvious to everyone that I was no longer "in the closet."

Yes, my career suffered, but so be it. I feel that what I am doing now, by spreading the word about the greatness of America and helping others to bring attention and awareness to the unbridled corruption in Washington, is much more important than appearing on a show. If God wills it, I will return to the big screen. If not, I have no regrets. This great country of ours is worth sacrificing for, and I will continue to fight for our freedom and liberty as long as I am able.

THE PSYCHOLOGY OF LABELS AND TRANSFORMATION

by GINA LOUDON

This hole in your heart is the shape of the one you lost and no one else can fit it.
—JEANETTE WINTERSON

The greatest gift a dad can give his daughter is to love her mother.
—ELAINE S. DALTON

People often ask why I studied psychology for all of those years, and my answer is simple: I wanted to fix the world so that no dads would ever leave their daughters again.

I knew that the loss of my father at a young age had massive impact on my life. Like every little girl, I have always wanted to be "Daddy's little girl." I never really was, and at this point, it is pretty clear that I never will be.

When I wrote about this at WND, and told the story of my dad's resentment of me today for my politics, some thought I was too harsh. Others thought he was terrible for letting politics come between us. I say neither is true. I will say it again in straight terms: My dad resents my work, and me for my work. More painful, he resents me for having children, because he is a supporter of "zero population growth." Although he is fine with late-term abortion, supports a one-world government, and thinks the church is too judgmental of people, if you ask me who influenced my activism the most, I would say my dad did. He believes the opposite of me on just about every issue. He gives a lot of his time and talents to Planned Parenthood. But he isn't a hateful man. He even goes on medical missions to Guatemala. He loves humanity and serves it fervently. I only hope I can serve my God as well as he serves his god of humanity. That doesn't make him horrible or hate-worthy. That makes him human, and sinful, just like me.

As I have thought about it over and over, I don't think it is our political differences that divide us as much as labels. He is pro-choice; I am pro-life. He is a Democrat; I have voted Republican. He is a statist; I am a conservative. He is on the left, and I am a right-winger. Or are we?

Labels can be insidious and deceptive. They are really more popular with children seeking to understand their world in the concrete operational stage of development, when it is hard for them to process information.

Those who actively engage in applying labels to political groups often have a covert agenda. Take the label "Tea Party." Few could tell you what the original term, T.E.A., actually stands for, but it is simply "taxed enough already."

While the majority of Americans would agree that they are overtaxed, those ignorant of the basis of the acronym might call the Tea Party dangerous, fringy, or extreme. But the elitist statists' attack on free-market groups goes much deeper. I would venture to say that they have a vendetta. It is worse than simply winning elections, and much, much deeper than party. I believe it is about dismantling the fundamental construction of America and using weak-minded, easily persuaded, low-information voters to do so.

If we are to be truly engaged, we must understand on what basis we engage. We must know the rulebook for Americans; that is, the US Constitution. More precisely, we must know the tools at our disposal to fight the war. Those tools are in the Bill of Rights. And the first step in fighting against the confusion of the rulebook is to fight against the imposed labels of the "left" on one side and the "right" on another, with "moderates" in the middle. None of those labels are correct.

The terms *left* and *right* come originally from the French monarchy. The concept was that those with the central form of government (the king) were on his right, so the term *right wing* meant those who stood with the monarchy. If you opposed the king, and stood for freedom or liberty from the monarchy, you were on the left. That seems to be the polar opposite of where we are today.

If the US Constitution is the basis of our republic, then the moderate, or centrist, should be the one who believes the most strongly in the US Constitution (as it is the center of the political frame). As elucidated recently by a man named Steven Maikoski in his 2013 book *Arguing for the Constitution*, the statists slap the "right wing" epithet on those who are really centrists when the pervading form of government is a constitutional republic. Those who wish to divorce the Bill of Rights and the US Constitution are guilefully using words and labels to distinguish themselves as the "noble freedom fighters" while eroding the personal freedoms inherent in the founding documents.

The statists regularly say that the conservatives are imposing their morality on the people. But they are the ones who want to keep writing new laws. And all those laws are an imposition of their view of morality on the people. As I wrote in a 2014 article for *WND Commentary*, "The theocracy is not that of the 'religious right' or the 'moral majority' or the 'political fringe' labels that the

American public has come to hysterically fear. The theocracy is that of political correctness. Political correctness is not accountable to the American people, nor will it defend them in a war, persecution, political tyranny or any other situation."[1]

For this reason, labels not only divide family, friends, and neighbors, I would argue that the statist-promulgated definition of political correctness is the most dangerous lie imposed on America to date.

CONCRETE DEFINITIONS BASED ON POLITICAL LOGIC

As I've done before, in my articles, I challenge those who fear morality or the "radical right-wing fringe" (who, as evidenced, aren't radical, or on the right, or on the fringe at all) to stand up for free speech and join forces with the constitutional centrists in this country who want to protect it. Stop being deceived by those who bully you into silence when the speech being restricted doesn't fit their agenda.

We see people who call themselves "leftists" or "progressives" defending the right to have pornography in libraries or for so-called artists to display utterly offensive works, all in the name of free speech—"speech" that is detrimental to young minds. But these same people will remain silent when someone is fined for standing up for his or her religious beliefs or prevented from praying silently in a school.

The proliferation of political correctness has real victims, just as pornography has victims. If you are for free speech, you should be for it everywhere. If you are against it, you shouldn't hide it. It's not a left or right thing. These labels are designed to create confusion and division. Instead someone who believes in big government is a "statist." Someone who believes in the US Constitution is a "constitutional centrist" or a "constitutional conservative." The rest are "on the fringe."

The sad truth is that the worst of the statist's labeling looks a lot like the slave plantations they claim to hate, and in some cases claim to be still fighting. I call their tactic of making people dependent and then using them for votes and protests "plantation politics."

As I wrote in my book *Ladies and Gentleman*, "They hand [money and free stuff] out like slave owners will, and call it social welfare. They subjugate the people and call them working people. They take away freedom and call it fairness. They emasculate men and call it equality. They steal from people and call it taxation. They steal even more, and call it dues. They own people, and call it organizing. They kill people, and call it choice. Would someone explain to me what is more palatable about this than the plantation they all claim to abhor?"[2]

The statists today see themselves as rebelling against the culture and traditions of the status quo. The problem is, once the "rebels" become the drivers of culture, they have also become the very thing they want to rebel against: the status quo. They all begin to think and look the same.

BEYOND LABELS, INTO THE PERSONAL

Sometimes journalists find the most fascinating interviews right under their noses. My dad and I are a family divided by labels, and I spend a lot of time trying to remind him that we do agree on some things. But when I don't talk to him for a while, I find him slipping deeper and deeper into the statist abyss.

I learned that to venture inside the radically statist, tyranny-endorsing mind-set, I only have to go as far as my own father. I love my dad and wanted all of my life to be the daughter that he wanted. I am the only child of two only children.

My dad left my mother when I was a little girl. He told me he was going on a ski trip, but instinctively I knew that was not true.

The day the door closed and my father left, I knew I would never, ever be the same. I remember running around my house, screaming and crying. With tears streaming down her face, my mom caught me in my exhaustion. When I woke up, I knew he was really gone.

My school hosted an annual father/daughter party on Father's Day, and I was dreading it so badly. There were no other children of divorced parents in my kindergarten class. I wanted to die. When the father/daughter party finally came, my grandpa went with me so I wouldn't be alone. The kids laughed at me and made fun of me because my "dad" looked so old.

My mother eventually remarried, and my father continued trying to find himself. He dated my teachers and my friends' mothers, and all of this made me very confused. I just wanted him to come home, and I wanted to be his little girl.

There were the plays he didn't see, the report cards he didn't read, and the holidays where I fantasized about a big, cuddly daddy who would wrap his big, strong arms around me, and hand me a little box filled with something shiny that said, "Daddy's Little Girl." The daddy of my dreams not only didn't act like my dad; he didn't look like him either.

I wanted the traditional dad, who came home from work and sang out, "Honey, I'm home!" as he set his briefcase on the table. Then I wanted him to scoop me up and swing me around and tell me how precious I was to him. I wanted him to buy me pretty dresses, because that is what I loved. I wanted a dad who would baby me and want to keep me little forever so I could always be his. But my dad just wanted me to grow up.

My dad was adopted by a kindly but busy doctor and his wife. Like me, my dad has severe ADHD, and he gave his adoptive mother a run for her money, even as a baby. Overwhelmed and impatient, she sent him away to military school at the tender age of three. I still have the teddy bear that he cuddled on those cold, dark nights at Missouri Military Academy. If the teddy bear was any sign, I knew my dad was capable of love. Heartbreakingly so.

My dad loves physics, sex, and politics, but not necessarily in that order. To this day, he keeps a physics textbook out on his kitchen table, so he can study it in his spare moments. He still works out nonstop, as he did when I was growing up, so he will look good for the ladies. My dad became a fan of Paul R. Ehrlich and Alfred Kinsey in the 1970s and never really changed politically since then. Dad's ideas of modesty (or the lack thereof) confused me. When he tried to teach me physics from the thickest textbook I had ever seen, he confused both of us. Sex and physics were two passions of my dad's that I couldn't understand. But politics, I could learn! I would find my way to be the daughter he always wanted, after all!

When we found ourselves together, working in his dental lab, we would talk politics. Our entire relationship became one of calmly debating politics together. That was the one and only place we ever connected, and the only way, outside of sports, that I felt his approval. Sometimes he would get very agitated with me, but that was only when I disagreed with him and stood my ground. Most of the time I went along with him, because I figured I was a kid and he was a dad, so he must know something I didn't know.

I met a political science major at a blood drive my freshman year. My mom was crazy for John. He was raised Christian Science. John was from a big family, something I had always wanted. He was brilliant, beautiful, athletic, and sincere. I knew I could trust him the moment I met him. I loved him. I could see him as a daddy for my children one day, if I could ever work up the courage to have children, and endure being such a disappointment to my dad.

My dad liked John. He was pro-choice, liked the United Nations, didn't like Reagan, wanted to save the planet, didn't care to "pollute the earth with kids," worked out nonstop, and loved to talk politics! He would win my dad for me! I wished.

At first my dad was so pleased with my marriage to John and our left-leaning lives that he offered us a partnership in his business! After a honeymoon across Europe, we came home and slapped my dad's favorite bumper sticker on our eco-car: "The ultimate pollution solution: Birth Control." (He coined the phrase and had bumper stickers made up.) We had traveled all over Europe, and we were now enlightened. We thought it was funny to have something so audacious on our car, and we enjoyed the shock on people's faces when they read it. We rationalized that those people were probably small-minded Christian types who didn't understand that people make pollution. They were probably idiots, and maybe my dad's sticker would shock them back into reality.

As we worked in my dad's company, things began to hit me, hard. One day I had an epiphany. In a definitive moment, after working for hours in his lab as he chided me for my conservative leanings, I lost control. Although my dad loved me, he simply didn't want to be around me if I disagreed with his politics. That was a pivotal moment for me. I realized that to have my dad, I had to deny my beliefs. I had to deny that I thought babies in the womb were alive; that I believed big government led to tyranny; and that I thought capitalism was not only better for people, but that it was biblical (2 Thessalonians 3:10). I realized that if I were going to "keep" my dad, I had to reject God.

I threw thousands of expensive, microscopic ball bearings I was inserting in my dad's latest medical instrument all over the lab in a desperate rage. I was lashing out not just at my father but at all the events that were perpetrated by the divorce. I had experienced so much growing up, and I decided, *I will not be owned!*

I left in tears, and my dad and I didn't speak for years.

That prompted my political transformation from a desire to be what my dad wanted me to be in an effort to win his approval, to a hard-core search for truth—religiously and politically.

In the years that followed, I rebelled horribly. I had children. And my husband converted from his Christian Science religion to become a bona fide born-again Calvinist. Every time I saw my husband tenderly loving on my daughters, I felt a pain deep in my soul. On the one hand, I was so happy for my girls to have the daddy I always wanted. On the other hand, their relationship was a constant reminder that I would never, ever be Daddy's little girl.

In years since, I have learned to love the dad God decided to give me. So much of what I enjoy about my life, I owe to him. I love my ability to think critically. God knows that came straight from him. I love my tendency to question the conventional. He taught me to search for what is true and not to believe something just because someone tells me it is so. My heart still aches each time I think of the rejection he experienced in his own life that made it so hard for him to love. I think of his adoption, and that has given me the passion and courage to adopt my own child, Samuel. I think of the abortions that my dad has selflessly funded in his belief that he is saving the world from more people that it cannot afford, and I thank God for life, and for the gift of marrying my husband, who has saved thousands of babies through his legislation in the Missouri Senate.

I thank God, the One my dad can't seem to believe in, for my dad.

My dad is probably horrified to know that it was the long days of working by his side in his lab, as we listened to Paul Harvey, that inspired my career in TV and radio. He probably hates it that it was the years of him criticizing and challenging me to debate him that made me confident to debate in the public arena. He probably wouldn't want to know that it was his own adoption—and his sad upbringing—that made me ardently pro-life. I think he would be shocked to know that my deep faith in God and my love for Jesus Christ are a direct result of his skepticism expressed to me so many times, and my tireless search for truth to test his doubts.

He might not mind knowing that it is his steadfast commitment to the parents I thought didn't do enough for him that made me loyal. And that it was his inability to be my dad in the ways I needed one, that prompted me to find a dedicated, loving father for my children.

My father is a self-made, wealthy man who gives most of his money to causes I fight. He despises my values and my work. I know that I am the epitome of his broken dreams, and that my life is a walking disappointment to him. I know he has to struggle to answer questions about family because he doesn't want to admit publicly that *his* daughter is on Fox News, or that he has five grandchildren. That doesn't bode well for the bumper sticker that still adorns his window.

My dad has taught me so much, though it isn't what he meant to teach me, I am sure.

PART 2

WHAT MAKES A WOMAN

4

HOLLYWOOD AND THE TRANSFORMATION OF OUR CULTURE

by MORGAN BRITTANY

> Those who do not study history are forced to get it from Hollywood.
> —ALLEN BARRA

THE '50S AND '60S

In the mid-1950s I entered the workforce. I was five years old, and one of my earliest and most vivid memories was standing under massive arc lights with the red eye of a CBS camera pointed at me.

I was appearing in a television show called *Playhouse 90*. The episode was titled "The Shape of the River," and it was about a man who returned to his hometown in the Midwest around the turn of the century because he wanted to return to the simpler ways of life and the comforts of home. I somehow wish that I could slip back to that soundstage at CBS and relive a gentler time.

Motion pictures and especially television during the early '50s and '60s primarily told stories of family, heroes, adventure, and fantasy. No matter what genre the television show, they spent thirty minutes or an hour resolving a conflict, and ended with an uplifting or meaningful message that you could take away with you. The majority of motion pictures were extravagant musicals, like *Singin' in the Rain* (1952), *Gypsy* (1962), and *The Sound of Music* (1965); comedies, with Doris Day, Rock Hudson, Bob Hope, and Lucille Ball; dramas and war movies, like *The Bridge on the River Kwai* (1957); and westerns, like *The Searchers* (1956), with John Wayne—all of which brought in huge audiences.

By the mid-1950s, however, there was a change brewing. After World War II the culture started to shift and America could see the seeds of change, first in motion pictures and then later in television.

During the first thirty to forty years in Hollywood, the content of motion pictures and radio programming could be contained and sent out to the public under the watchful eye of the studio mogul. In the early days of film, the studios were run, by and large, by self-made immigrants with a love for America and its values, and they wanted to spread that message through their work. Men like Louis B. Mayer, who ran MGM, and Jack Warner, who was in control of Warner Bros., had their fingers on the pulse of America and knew what an audience wanted. Films like *The Wizard of Oz* (1939), *The Grapes of Wrath* (1940), *Of Mice and Men* (1939), and *Gone with the Wind* (1939) were spectacularly produced and stand the test of time. Just a few powerful men controlled Hollywood, and yes, they were in business to make money, but they also wanted to keep their integrity. MGM's slogan was "Do it right . . . make it big . . . give it class!" and that was the general rule in early Hollywood.

After a film was finished, it was scrutinized by the head of the studio and other executives. If there was anything that pushed the boundaries or overstepped the line of morality, it ended up on the cutting room floor or was reshot. In 1939, the use of the word *damn* in *Gone with the Wind* caused a major controversy. The studios made product that was acceptable for everyone to see, young and old, and they made sure that their stamp of approval was given before any film was released.

I was very fortunate to grow up on the back lots of the major studios. I went to school at Warner Bros., MGM, Universal and 20th Century Fox and learned about life at an early age. As a child performer, you are never *really* a child, just a small person in an adult world. You were expected to perform and behave in a professional, mature manner, always prepared and always ready. That was your job, you were being well paid, and nothing but the best was expected. It was not easy, and many young stars had difficulty with it. The world was a different place then, and the publicity machine at the studios quickly extinguished any scandal affecting a star. Stars and performers were to be protected at all cost, because any tarnishing of their images would destroy their careers. Today, the reverse is true. The more scandal, the more the reward.

When I entered the Hollywood world in 1956, the studio system was beginning to crumble. The Mayers, Warners, Cohns, and Zanucks were losing their grip and were being replaced by young blood that had different attitudes about where Hollywood should be heading. Television was a major force to be reckoned with, and the new studio execs felt that in order to get people back in the theaters (paying customers), they had to offer something new and edgy that television couldn't.

Television shows like *Father Knows Best*, *I Love Lucy*, *Gunsmoke*, *Lassie*, and *The Dick Van Dyke Show* were all serving up fare that the entire family could enjoy and relate to, where they could gather around the television set and watch for free in the comfort of their own homes. Maybe life wasn't really like what was portrayed on that little screen, but we all wanted to believe that it was, and we tried our best to follow those examples. Whether it was comedy, drama, science fiction, or variety, television was *entertainment* that the entire family could view together.

The first signs of a major cultural shift took root in the 1950s. It was a time of postwar affluence, the baby boom, the birth of fast food, the all-electric home, and the first credit card. There were 10.5 million television sets in homes across America in 1950, and the majority of viewers were families and older people.

This left a vacuum when it came to the emerging youth in the country. Young people were breaking out on their own, finding more freedom than past generations, and they were looking for their own path to follow. The path out of the '40s into the '50s led to rebellion and Hollywood was there to stoke the fire.

Hollywood gave young people what they were looking for in the form of the antihero. New stars emerged, like James Dean, Paul Newman, Marlon Brando, and Marilyn Monroe. They took over for the establishment stars of the 1930s and '40s, like Tyrone Power Sr., Robert Taylor, and Shirley Temple. Films like *The Wild One* (1953), *Rebel Without a Cause* (1957), and *Peyton Place* (1957) gave rise to new fashion and images of dangerous behavior. Even though the Legion of Decency condemned many of these films as being too bold and for pushing agendas, Hollywood and the new studio heads forged ahead. They sensed blood in the water and made more and more product that pushed new boundaries. They created beautiful yet troubled characters that teens could emulate. They created and exploited youth as dangerous, sexy, defiant, in ways that had never been done before, and the eager audiences molded their lifestyles to mirror those that they saw on-screen.

The studios started putting out films that were taboo just a few years earlier. Instead of just seeing uplifting, heartwarming stories of heroes and success, life was being portrayed as it often really was. Stories were told about battles with alcoholism (*The Lost Weekend*, 1945), extramarital affairs (*The Apartment*, 1960), and family crisis (*East of Eden*, 1955). Even if their own lives were not reflected in these films, young people were being awakened to the darker and seedier side of life.

The emergence of rock and roll in the 1950s and early '60s was also a boon for filmmakers. They tapped into the fact that young moviegoers didn't want to see films that would appeal to their parents. They wanted to see and hear the latest stars singing their latest songs in films that promoted a young, carefree lifestyle. Some of the films were harmless enough, with stars like Annette Funicello and Sandra Dee alongside Frankie Avalon and Pat Boone, but others pushed the exploitation button and used actresses like Jayne Mansfield to establish an over-the-top, sexualized image of the American woman. Mansfield's portrayal of the dumb blonde sex symbol in *The Girl Can't Help It* cemented the stereotype of the big-busted airhead. The film's producers saw a huge success with this film by incorporating seventeen hit songs by popular artists into the storyline.

By the end of the decade, in all its forms, the youth market was worth $10 billion a year, and Hollywood wanted a big bite out of that. Like the proverbial frog in the pot of boiling water, the heat was being turned up ever so slightly, and little by little, old ways of thinking were falling by the wayside. Hollywood turned the burner up throughout the entire decade of the '50s, and by the time 1960 rolled around, it was too late to jump out.

THE '60S AND '70S

Many times during my childhood, I wanted to stay in the comforting arms of the make-believe world with Mr. Dillon on *Gunsmoke*, or walk down the main street of Mayberry on *The Andy Griffith Show*. That was my life, and I wanted to live in that world, but at the end of the day, the lights went out, the makeup came off, and you walked into the real world. The 1950s weren't all rosy, by any means, but they were nothing compared to the '60s. The 1950s had its share of problems: racial inequality, gender inequality, and other issues that needed to be addressed. Maybe things were not glowing all the time, but there was still a sense of goodness in most people. They were still times when a contract was a handshake, a promise was kept, and building character and a good reputation was a thing to be admired.

Up until the early '60s, I wasn't aware of a change in the type of work I was doing, but as I grew older, I started to sense a change—a shift, so to speak—in the subtle messages being hidden in scripts that I would read. By the late '60s there was a definite unease and discontent permeating our culture.

It is almost universal that most people pinpoint the major shift in our culture and society to right after the death of "Camelot"; that is, John F. Kennedy, his presidency, and the image of his fairy-tale life.

Those of us who remember Kennedy's assassination know exactly where we were and how we felt that day. The nation stood still, just as it did on 9/11, and things were never the same again.

In Hollywood during the 1960s, filmmakers began to push the envelope even more than they had in the '50s, planting the seeds of ideas that would grow in this new world, cautiously at first, and then with more vigor. They had tested the waters and realized the extent of their power of influence. Hollywood had always been on the front lines in manipulating minds and values because it created fantasy lifestyles that people wanted to emulate.

In the '60s, while President Kennedy's Camelot was in full swing, the most popular films were still romantic comedies starring the likes of Doris Day and Rock Hudson, and cutting-edge spy films, like James Bond's *Goldfinger*, were emerging. There were big-budget musicals, like *My Fair Lady*, *The Music Man*, *Can-Can*, and, of course, *Camelot*. Disney also had its niche audience and was faithful to its image of family values. If families and the older generation went out to the movies, Disney movies were what they wanted to see. Television was full of sitcoms about families, or westerns like *Bonanza*, the majority with positive messages.

After Kennedy's death, the antiestablishment movement took over in Hollywood. The progressive influence inched its way into the studio system and tried to push out the remaining old guard, who tried to continue selling feel-good films. Instead of making films and television shows that catered to the whole family, scripts were skewed even more toward the youth culture. In the 1960s, 80 percent of the moviegoing population were between the ages of sixteen and twenty-five. The progressives in Hollywood knew that if you wanted to make a statement and change the political culture, it had to be done with the youth.

Films were packed with even more social commentary than had been seen in the 1950s. Boundaries were crossed without hesitation, and old taboos were thrown out. For example, *Bonnie and Clyde* was promoted with the slogan "They're young . . . they're in love . . . and they kill people." Following on the heels of violent films such as that, sexual boundaries were tested in such films as *The Graduate*, which became one of the highest-grossing films of the decade.

History was being rewritten through films about the settling of the West. Films such as *Little Big Man* gave a different perspective on history, and it made little difference to the filmmaker whether the truth was told or not. War films tended to play into the antiwar movement of the time, focusing on the harshness, not the heroism.

Little by little, things on-screen became less shocking. Violence that would have made an audience cringe ten years earlier was mainstream. Nudity was inserted into love scenes, and graphic sex was becoming commonplace. Drug use and disrespect were considered the norm and glamorized in films like *Easy Rider*. The antihero was now someone to be worshipped and admired.

The reality of the dangerous world we lived in entered our lives through our TV sets during the 1960s. Not only did we see the first live murder on our screens when Jack Ruby killed Lee Harvey Oswald, but we were given, through moving images, daily updates of the Cuban missile crisis, the threat from the Soviet Union, and race riots. The world was coming into our homes in a different way than it had during World War II. It used to be that the problems of the world were far away; now they seemed so much closer. The news media reported their point of view with little or no question.

The media focused heavily on social issues during the 1960s. It was the beginning of the radical movements that took over society during this period. There was discontent with the establishment; women felt dissatisfied with their lives and joined the ranks of the feminist movement; antiwar was the cause célèbre for the youth of the day. Drugs, sex, and rock and roll had no penalties or repercussions. Anger overtook the streets, with riots and protesting, and violence was accepted as a way to make your point.

Voices like those of Martin Luther King Jr., who wanted to instill calm, were extinguished in the blink of an eye by a senseless act of violence, and we watched it all on our television sets. The American body count during the Vietnam War became background noise at our dinner tables. The media were in a frenzy, covering every bit of news with eyewitness reporters and cameramen.

Hollywood continued to mirror what it was seeing, and upped the ante. Not only did it cover the issues being talked about through the news, but it began to dig up and bring to life on the screen subjects that had only been whispered about. New films dealt with interracial relationships (*A Patch of Blue*) and the feminist movement (*The Group*). Difficult subject matter was addressed in brilliant films such as *To Kill A Mockingbird*, but the overall tone was dark. Foreign films were making their mark on the American cinema, and more taboo subjects were being introduced to audiences from foreign shores. British cinema introduced the *Angry Young Man* theme, where harsh language, sexual dysfunction, and anger portrayed the plight of alienated youth.

In 1962 one of the most controversial films of the decade was released: *Lolita.* It was the story of an academic who marries a woman to get close to her underage nymphet daughter. This film paved the way and opened the door to the acknowledgment of underage love affairs. It created an uproar at the time, but today is met with nothing more than a shrug.

The '60s hit America like a whirlwind in more ways than one. It was a cultural upheaval that battered like a tsunami. By the end of the decade, films and some television shows had pushed the envelope so far that the public was saturated. They could see the effect the Hollywood machine was having on their children and families. The Motion Picture Association of America was now rating films so that parents could monitor what their children were seeing. A backlash was beginning because people had seen enough sex, drugs, nudity, violence, and perversions. They needed to pull back and were looking for some kind of relief outside of the wonderful world of Disney.

In 1968 Lucille Ball had the answer. The owner of Desilu Productions/Paramount Pictures, she had acquired the rights to a book that she wanted to produce and make into a film. That project was called *Yours, Mine and Ours.* All of Lucy's advisers warned her against making the film, saying it just was too old-fashioned for "today's" world, and she would lose money. She was adamant and told them that was exactly *why* the film should be made. No sex, no nudity, no bad language, no violence, just good old-fashioned family values. She had made up her mind.

Lucy got Henry Fonda on board, as well as Tom Bosley and Van Johnson. The children were all cast as unknowns. I was one of them. I played Henry Fonda's daughter Louise Beardsley; I was about fifteen.

This film will always be a treasured memory for me, not only because I got to go to work every day with Lucy Ball and Henry Fonda, but because it taught me a work ethic that I carry with me to this day. It also gave me the faith and courage to believe that you can change things for the better if you are passionate about it.

The week the film opened in 1968, Lucy and all of the kids appeared on *The Ed Sullivan Show* in New York. We were there to sing the theme song and give people a taste of what the film was about. At the premiere we all sat and waited to see what the New York artistic crowd would say. The audience laughed, applauded, and gave Lucy a standing ovation. The film was a hit, and the following week, *Variety* magazine declared, "They Still Love Lucy!" The film was a smash, and Lucy knew it.

America was waiting for a change, a breath of fresh air after a decade filled with upheaval and shifting values. It was a simple film with simple values that appealed to the heart of the country. With the success of *Yours, Mine and Ours*, you would think Hollywood and the media would finally wake up.

THE '70S AND BEYOND

In the 1970s another cultural shift took place. The Hollywood progressives had overplayed their hand and pushed the limits too far. Audiences dwindled at the local theaters, and more people were staying home, in front of their television sets. Studio back lots were being sold for housing developments and shopping centers. Film libraries, costume departments, and props were on the auction block. Hollywood was in decline and falling fast.

Television was offering wholesome, somewhat mindless entertainment, but it was comfortable for the American audiences. They loved the antics of *The Brady Bunch, The Monkees, Batman,* and *Love, American Style*. Even *Laugh-In* was a family show that made folks feel good. The television executives knew what the American people wanted, and even though many of them leaned left, they were smart enough to give it to them. They pulled back and waited for the next opportunity to push their agendas.

Wholesome shows like *Little House on the Prairie* and *The Waltons* were garnering huge audiences. The public wanted values and morals in their living room, and the networks bought into that market. Never to give up on their progressive push, however, they peppered the airwaves with just enough material to plant more seeds into the minds of young viewers. *All in the Family* was one show that broke the mold and was massively successful for CBS. The show was centered on a working-class bigot and his family. It examined subjects that had been taboo on television in the past, like racism, homosexuality, women's lib, rape, miscarriage, and breast cancer. The brilliance of the producers centered around the casting of the show. They knew that if the characters weren't lovable and funny— many times making fun of themselves—the messages would never be accepted. The subject matter had to be presented in a way that was palatable to the audience without being offensive or shocking. No doubt about it, the creators of the show were brilliant.

In contrast to *Family, The Cosby Show* tackled more of the subjects that we had seen in the early days of television. Family issues, kids growing up, and balancing family and jobs were all dealt with in a way that taught a lesson. It was the first show of its kind where an upper middle-class black family was seen without the "color" label. Audiences of all races, creeds, and colors loved to tune in and watch the Huxtable family deal with issues that they themselves were going through. It was a huge step toward blurring the color lines in this country and had a magic touch with the public.

The feature filmmakers also did an about-face in the late '70s and early '80s. Instead of continuing their losing streak, they made an abrupt shift back to the values that had succeeded in making America great. All at once, films like *Star Wars*, *Raiders of the Lost Ark*, *Superman*, *E.T.*, and *Grease* were cleaning up at the box office, breaking records that hadn't been seen in years. Heroes were making a resurgence. Rocky became a character you could root for, and Harry Callahan in *Dirty Harry* was the cop that always got the bad guy.

Progressive Hollywood had to grit its teeth during the Reagan years. As much as they wanted to push their agendas, the money just wasn't there. Big corporations were buying up the studios, and their goal was to make the highest-grossing movies they could. Only a handful of moviegoers were interested in seeing films about abortion, crazy priests, and psychotic military officers. The corporate bosses wanted pure entertainment.

Hollywood looks at the highest-grossing films of the year, and they aren't blind to the fact that wholesome, family movies top the box office every time. If you look at the top-grossing films of all time, the majority of them are family or values films. A major shock hit the film world when Mel Gibson's *Passion of the Christ* was released. It stunned the Hollywood elite by breaking box office records.

The door to a dysfunctional culture cracked open again in the 1990s. We watched in real time the murder trial of O. J. Simpson. With nonstop coverage, day after day the grisly details were laid out for us, and people were riveted to their television screens. Bill Clinton brought sex, cheating, and lying back to the forefront and laid it at our feet. However, that wasn't a movie; it was reality. Every day the news would cover the sexual details of the affair between Monica Lewinsky and the president. We learned more than we ever wanted to about cigars, oral sex, and stains on a blue dress. But when the president of the United States could flat-out lie to the American people and get away with it, that was a game changer. It suddenly gave carte blanche to everyone else. It taught young people that they could lie their way out of anything; after all, the president of the United States did! It also made oral sex more acceptable; after all, it wasn't really sex. That opened the door for teens all over America, as oral sex parties became popular even among middle schoolers. Rape and sexual harassment were acceptable if the woman was slutty. Cheating on your wife was no big deal, after all, Hillary stood by her man and accepted it. Bad behavior was being rewarded at an unprecedented level, and the more scandalous, the greater the benefit. Our leaders were teaching that if you attained power, you could get away with anything.

We have continued on this downward trajectory for over twenty years now. With the advent of reality television, people began degrading and humiliating themselves to a degree unimaginable even twenty-five years ago. Now fame has become the ultimate goal in life. When a teen girl tries to get pregnant in order to win a spot on the reality show *Teen Mom*, you know we are in trouble. Today, there is nothing too disgusting or crass as long as you become famous for it. Live a lifestyle like Snooki, and they will pay you thirty-five thousand dollars to speak at Rutgers University!

Alongside the pop culture arose the gangsta culture, which is particularly dangerous. It has succeeded in making profanity normal and the degradation of women admirable, and it has brought sex down to a level not seen since Neanderthals. By the way, grinding and "twerking" is not dancing by any stretch of the imagination.

Violence is worshipped, and life is cheap. Young people brought up without values and supervision have no qualms about randomly killing someone just because they are bored. Violent video games have deadened people's sensitivity to the point that they think nothing of grabbing a weapon and creating a massacre.

Unfortunately, when it is over, you can't hit the reset button and bring the victims back to life again.

I understand that change is inevitable, and that we can't go back to the good old days and live in a bubble. But are we changing for the better? I think the answer is no. Instead of becoming more intelligent and genteel and living our lives with dignity and honor, we are becoming more coarse and vulgar. The world seems to be upside down. Our leaders mock faith and religious values. Our Judeo-Christian foundation is being dragged through the courts and extinguished at every turn.

When there is no fear of consequences in this life or the hereafter, chaos is the order of the day. We don't think twice about breaking the Ten Commandments because they don't mean anything any-more. With a good lawyer it's easy to get away with lying, cheating, stealing, and even murder, and the profits to be made with film and book deals after the trial are staggering. As long as *the ends justify the means,* then it is okay. The seduction of power and fame has now become more powerful than integrity and morality.

As an optimist I want to believe that there will be a tipping point when things begin to turn around. There is an ebb and flow to this country, and if you look at our history, things have challenged us many, many times. The United States has always triumphed over injustices. Good has always trumped evil, and I want to believe that it will again.

I only hope and pray that this time we have not gone too far. I don't want some filmmaker someday to preview a film called *The Decline and Fall of America.*

5

ISSUES THAT *REALLY* MATTER TO WOMEN, AND WHY

by ANN-MARIE MURRELL

Hate is the force that gives the left meaning. It isn't hope that animates its leaders and thinkers, but the darker side of human nature that calls on them to destroy and to kill. . . . The left finds its identity not in its utopian visions, but in the things and people it wishes to destroy. Only by knowing what they hate, do its followers know who they are.[1] —DANIEL GREENFIELD

Beginning with the 2012 elections and continuing today, progressives everywhere have proclaimed that Republicans not only hate women, but that they have also waged a war against them. Led by mega progressive George Soros's MoveOn.org, many low-information voters claim this is one of the main reasons they voted for Barack Obama—twice.

From the website Stop the War on Women:

The campaign to Stop the War on Women needs your voice. Tell Republicans no.

- *No* to taking away the rights and freedoms of American women.
- *No* to threatening the health of millions of women and their families.
- *No* to sneak attacks on women's right to choose.[2]

Then the website gives an update on how Congressman Cliff Stearns (R-FL), chair of a House oversight subcommittee, wanted to investigate what they call "one of the most important providers of health care for American women": Planned Parenthood.

Make no mistake: the entire so-called war on women that the GOP is supposedly waging is mostly about Planned Parenthood and the left's fears that their moneymaking abortion machine could someday lose its billions in government funding. It doesn't matter that Planned Parenthood has been involved in scandals and corruption—including an undercover video by Live Action.org that proved Planned Parenthood was willing and able to do late-term abortions based on sex selection.[3]

From Lila Rose at the *Daily Caller*: "Each year, Planned Parenthood receives hundreds of millions of dollars from you, the taxpayer—and the total is rising. This past year, Planned Parenthood got $542 million from the government (i.e., from you and me), which accounts for almost half (45%) of the abortion chain's budget. Abortions at Planned Parenthood are rising, while other services are falling.[4]

And while Obama's 2013 sequester cut hundreds of millions from our military, special education, and the National Park Services, Planned Parenthood hasn't lost a dime of its $542 million funding per year.

"Planned Parenthood is flush with cash," Rose wrote, "having reported excess revenue of $87.4 million and $1.2 billion in total assets last year. Cecile Richards, Planned Parenthood's CEO, makes nearly $400,000 a year. And yet the biggest abortion provider in America somehow still calls itself a non-profit."

StopTheWarOnWomen.com proclaims, "Republicans not only want to reduce women's access to abortion care, they're actually trying to *redefine rape*. After a major backlash, they promised to stop. But they haven't yet. Shocker."[5]

(By the way, I love how they added the word *care*, as if abortion has anything to do with health care, but I digress.)

Because I'm sick to death of the left claiming they are "victims" here in America, I wanted to give them a little reality check as to what a real World War on Women is all about. And it has nothing to do with not getting free birth control pills and condoms.

WAR ON WOMEN: AFGHANISTAN

Afghanistan was rated by the Revolutionary Association of the Women of Afghanistan (RAWA), a political organization of Afghan women fighting for human rights and social justice, as the number one worst place in the world to be born a woman. (Sorry, progressives. Despite how victimized you feel by the evil GOP, America didn't make the list.)

Although the War in Afghanistan removed the Taliban, according to RAWA.org, the improvement for women is only limited to certain parts of the country. "In other areas," the website states, "the incidence of rape and forced marriage is on the rise again, and most women continue to wear the burqa out of fear for their safety."[6]

Blogger and political activist Pamela Geller writes, "[E]nding abuse of women is a huge challenge in a patriarchal society where traditional practices include child marriage, giving girls away to settle debts or pay for their relatives' crimes, and so-called honour killings of girls seen as disgracing their families."[7]

WAR ON WOMEN: THE DEMOCRATIC REPUBLIC OF THE CONGO (DRC)

Congo, the number two worst place to be born a woman, was called the "rape capital of the world" by the UN. According to a

US study, more than four hundred thousand women are raped in Congo each year.

"Rights activists say militia groups and soldiers target all ages, including girls as young as three and elderly women," the survey reports. "They are gang raped, raped with bayonets and some have guns shot into their vaginas."[8]

But yeah, American progressives have to fight the evil GOP to get their free pap smears from Planned Parenthood.

WAR ON WOMEN: EGYPT

Within hours after the Obama administration cheered the ousting of former President Hosni Mubarak, CBS reporter Lara Logan was brutally gang-raped in the streets of Cairo. There was an immediate whitewashing about what actually happened to her, with reports that Logan was simply "groped" and beaten.[9] (Didn't want to spoil Obama's victory laps, right?)

Years later, the public rapes continue to tarnish the image of the "kinder, gentler Muslim Brotherhood," despite efforts by the MB's (aided by the Obama administration's Islamic PR machine). Of course, instead of trying to arrest the rapists, as we do here, in "imperialistic" America, the raped women of Egypt are being told it's their fault for being out in public. Police general Adel Abdel Maqsoud Afifi said, "Sometimes a girl contributes 100 percent to her own raping when she puts herself in these conditions."[10]

Forty-two-year-old journalist Hania Moheeb recently spoke out about her rape, recounting in a television interview that a group of men surrounded her and other women. They were stripped and violated for over three hours. Another rape victim said no one came to her rescue because the men told people she had a bomb strapped to her abdomen.[11]

The United States is (finally) taking action, with Congresswoman Ilena Ros-Lehtinen (R-FL) in the lead. As reported by Lydia Goodman of PolitiChicks.tv, Rep. Ros-Lehtinen and eighteen sponsors introduced House Resolution 416, "a bill that would limit specific military and economic aid to Egypt if certain standards are not met by the current government."[12]

We'll have to wait and see if the Obama administration does the right thing with this or not.

WAR ON WOMEN: CHINA

From 1971 to today, a "one child per family" rule has been strictly enforced in China. The Chinese government admitted that over the past four decades, 336 million babies have been aborted, some forcibly. If you're unsure what "forcibly" means, a story from March 22, 2013, came out of China in which a woman was discovered by authorities to be seven months pregnant. Apparently officials were tipped off that the woman and her husband already had their quota child, so they took the mother to the local hospital, injected her uterus with a potent chemical solution to induce the abortion, and two days later their seven-month-old (dead) baby emerged. The father took a picture of the dead infant, which has been circulating all over the social networking world.[13]

Supposedly China had banned late-term abortions, but apparently this is a bendable rule when someone dares to get pregnant more than once.

(Progressives, is this really the direction you want Planned Parenthood to go in America?)

WAR ON WOMEN: PAKISTAN

Unlike poor American women having to come up with change to pay for their own birth control, Pakistani woman have to deal with things like acid attacks, child and forced marriage, and punishment or retribution by stoning or other physical abuse.

Divya Bajpai at the International HIV/Aids Alliance said, "Pakistan has some of the highest rates of dowry murder, so-called honor killings and early marriage."[14]

According to Pakistan's human rights commission, as many as one thousand women and girls die in honor killings annually.[15]

These attacks, by the way, are double-edged swords for Pakistani women. Long after the physical pain is gone, the mental anguish lasts a lifetime. Physical attacks are usually inflicted on women for a reason—lying, cheating, and adultery—bringing "shame" to a family. So most women choose not to report their attacks to the corrupt police at all, and instead live the most miserable lives imaginable.

This list could go on and on—but let's get back to America.

Progressives, if you really care about women's rights as you claim you do, look a little farther than your own comfortable, safe bedrooms. Stop crying over having to come up with a few extra dollars to pay for your birth control—and/or abortions, if you must. Instead, you should start shedding tears and using your vast activist skills for the women who are actually waging a real war, struggling just to stay alive and exist in the world—and while you're at it, get your damned priorities in line.

BEAUTY PAGEANTS, DUCK DYNASTY, AND "TOLERANCE"

As a former Miss Texas contestant, I can tell you firsthand that by the time you see a televised beauty pageant, it is merely the end result of more than a year's worth of work. You can't simply enter a major pageant; you first have to win preliminary pageants to even qualify to compete in the finals. So having won several local crowns, I entered the Miss Lake o' the Pines pageant soon after graduating high school. Because it was a preliminary to Miss Texas, the competition was fierce. As long as they qualify, girls from anywhere in the state can compete in a preliminary. I wasn't expected to win; some of the girls competing were much more experienced, polished, and older than I was—but probably to the dismay of the pageant directors, I somehow managed to win.

Almost the moment the crown was placed on my head, the pageant directors went to work on me. Every day before I left for college, I met with my Miss Lake o' the Pines team: two directors, one manager, and a dress designer–stylist. I had a nonstop schedule full of public appearances, makeup and hair consultations, interview coaching, and shopping trips back and forth to Dallas. Every weekend of my freshman year, my team came to North Texas State to accompany me to various pageants and special events. I often had to walk through my dorm in full pageant regalia—which didn't make me very popular, by the way.

This might sound like fun to some, but it was extremely stressful trying to keep up with both my college and pageant responsibilities. I was scheduled to meet with an etiquette coach on a weekly basis (which I rarely did because she scared me to death). Despite the fact that I was only eighteen and very thin, I had to do torturous strength-building exercises a few hours a day for swimsuit competition—including relearning how to walk and stand because, according to their "experts," my spine didn't line up exactly right, so I had to cheat out my shoulder blade a bit. I attended (and sometimes performed in and/or judged) smaller preliminary pageants all over Texas, with fittings and shopping trips in between. And of course, I had to keep up with news and politics on a daily basis in preparation for the all-important interview segment.

Just like a sports team, if you have a strong coaching staff, as I did, by the time you get to the actual Super Bowl of pageants, everyone in the industry knows ahead of time who the VIP contestants are. They know your strengths and weaknesses, and since judges aren't sequestered, they, too, know who all of the contestants are before they ever hit the stage.

One thing many people don't know about state and national pageants is that the actual competition occurs over the course of four or five days. The year I competed in Miss Texas, there were sixty-two girls, divided into three groups. Each group competed on different nights in evening gown, swimsuit, and talent, with interviews spread throughout the days. On the night of the actual televised pageant, audience favorites had already been chosen, and everyone involved knew who the clear front-runners were.

I'm mentioning all of this because of Carrie Prejean, Miss California 2009. By the time the world watched her on television, competing in the Miss USA pageant, she had already won her preliminaries. She had worked a year (as I did) to win her state title (which I did not). Once Carrie won the state title, she underwent a full year of annoyingly grueling work, prepping for Miss USA. After hundreds of interviews, parade riding, charity work, media appearances, and that final week of preliminary competitions, the finalists were unofficially chosen long before the televised pageant.

Everyone in the entire pageant world knew who Carrie Prejean was, including the celebrity judges.

For all intents and purposes, Prejean was on track to win not only the Miss USA pageant but also the Miss Universe pageant. She was by far one of the most beautiful contestants; she was an audience favorite, and most important, she had that extra "sparkle" and charisma needed to capture America's attention. The only thing Carrie Prejean didn't have on her side was one judge: a gay activist named Perez Hilton, famous for his vicious and trashy (but strangely popular) celebrity gossip website.

When Perez Hilton asked Carrie Prejean his gotcha question,

her pageant career—and her entire life, for that matter—was about to change forever. Perez knew who Carrie was long before she stood in front of him on that stage. He knew her worldview and her Christian stance on the issues via any number of interviews she had conducted throughout the years. Perez used his question as a weapon to further his personal agenda and his career, and to bring him the national fame and attention he seemed desperately to long for. Yes, it was random that Carrie drew Perez's name out of a fishbowl—but his question to her was not.[16]

"The question I came up with for the interview portion of Miss USA tonight is SO good!!" Hilton tweeted to his followers before the event.

Knowing who Carrie Prejean was, Perez asked her: "Vermont recently became the fourth state to legalize same-sex marriage. Do you think every state should follow suit? Why or why not?"

On national television and in front of the entire world, Carrie Prejean had to make an immediate decision: either give the politically correct answer and win the pageant, or stand by her personal convictions and lose. She chose the latter when she said: "I think it's great Americans are able to choose one or the other. We live in a land that you can choose same-sex marriage or opposite marriage. And you know what, in my country, in my family, I think that I believe that a marriage should be between a man and a woman. No offense to anybody there, but that's how I was raised and that's how I think it should be, between a man and a woman."

With the cameras steadied on Perez Hilton's face, he gave a smarmy, disgusted, yet almost gleeful look. You could hear a few boos in the audience, but mostly there was applause.

Carrie Prejean was chosen first runner-up.

The morning after, Hilton began blogging about what he called the "worst answer in pageant history." He began a major trash campaign against Carrie Prejean, and in one of his most innocuous interviews, he told ABC News he was "floored" by her answer. "I haven't said this before, but to her credit, I applaud her for her honesty. However, she is not a politician, she's a hopeful Miss USA. Miss USA should represent everyone. Her answer alienated millions of gay and lesbian Americans, their families and their supporters."[17] Mostly, Hilton seemed giddy by all the attention he was getting.

Ultimately, there were lawsuits and smear campaigns and ugliness on every account—but all of it was simply because Carrie Prejean gave an honest answer about her personal beliefs instead of telling a lie.

Fast-forward to 2014 and Drew Magary's *GQ* interview with *Duck Dynasty* patriarch Phil Robertson. After spending hours talking with Robertson and his family, Magary absolutely knew what type of answer he would get when he asked Phil Robertson, "What, in your mind, is sinful?"

Like Carrie Prejean before him, Phil Robertson answered his question honestly, based on his personal Christian beliefs. After giving his (albeit crude) thoughts on homosexuality, he added, "We never, ever judge someone on who's going to heaven, hell. That's the Almighty's job. We just love 'em, give 'em the good news about Jesus—whether they're homosexuals, drunks, terrorists. We let God sort 'em out later, you see what I'm saying?"[18]

At first I wasn't sure what Magary's agenda was, or if he had one at all. As a successful writer and author, he certainly knew that Robertson's statement about gay sex was pure journalistic gold. However, any thoughts I might have had about an "unbiased" interview were erased when I read Magary's follow-up article for Deadspin, titled, "The Devil and Phil Robertson: My Day with *Duck Dynasty*." The man obviously has a deep contempt for Southerners—especially the Christian conservative types. Magary wrote:

I don't agree with Phil's politics, and I have a lot of gay relatives and colleagues who would bristle at Phil's "hate the sin, love the sinner" view of homosexuality. They've had to hear that [stuff] for years. But I still like Phil and found him to be an otherwise decent fellow. I think it's all right to think that, and I think it's all right to hope that whatever fuss arises out of his comments—it's happening already—will soften him a bit toward what he believes to be wicked behavior. Consider this my own version of "hate the sin, love the sinner."[19]

So there ya go.

Although Carrie Prejean has long moved away from her pageant years, the antigay stigma will follow her forever. It will be the same with Phil Robertson. But for both, their strong family ties and their unfaltering faith in God are their saving grace, protecting them from all the haters of the world. And yes, the gay agenda thought police are all about intolerance and hate. They sadly believe they have to do whatever it takes to force people into agreeing with (and/or approving of) their lifestyle 100 percent.

What they seem to forget—or choose to ignore—is that using a public forum to silence *anyone's* beliefs, lifestyle, and/or personal choices, is the opposite of everything America was founded on. And trying to block out all opposing opinions using public bullying tactics and psychological warfare is literally the very definition of *intolerant*:

1:    unable or unwilling to endure
2a: unwilling to grant equal freedom of expression especially in religious matters
  b: unwilling to grant or share social, political, or professional rights : bigoted[20]

Ironically, the provocation, closed-mindedness, harassment, and, yes, intolerance that the gay community is forcing upon the

Judeo-Christian community is precisely what they once professed they were fighting to end.

THE CELEBRITY WAR AGAINST CONSERVATIVES

Sarah Palin. The name alone invokes an almost visceral emotion in people on both the left and the right. There are few tepid Palin people; folks either adore her or they hate her.

In an article called "Why the Left Hates Sarah Palin," Evan Sayet wrote:

> If Democrats disagreed with Ms. Palin on the issues that would be one thing. But they don't merely "disagree" with her, they hate her and they hate her without caring one whit about where she stands on the issues. They hate her because she is living proof that everything about the Democratic Party narrative is a lie and for this reason she cannot be allowed to be liked—because if Democrats liked her, they might actually listen to her policies.[21]

If you're not sure this is true, ask any number of progressive celebrities what they think of Sarah Palin, including Bill Maher, who famously called her a "dumb twat"[22] and called her children "inbred weirdoes."[23] MSNBC's Martin Bashir ultimately resigned after calling Palin "America's resident dunce" and suggesting that someone should "defecate in her mouth and urinate in her eyes."[24]

In my opinion, the following 2008 statement from then Alaska governor Sarah Palin summarizes why progressives were so frightened of her. From the start, Palin openly declared herself to be a woman of God: "I knew early on that the smartest thing for me to do was to work hard, do the best that I can, make wise decisions based on good information in front of me. And then put my life, get myself on a path that could be dedicated to God and ask Him what I should do next. That will be the position I will be in as long as I'm on earth—that is, seeking the right path that God would have laid out for me."[25]

Terrifying, right? Well, to antireligious, anti-traditional progressives, Palin's words were like a crucifix to a vampire (or progressive atheist). Add to that the fact that Sarah Palin dearly loves her family in a very traditional, old-fashioned kind of way, and that's a scary combination for forward-thinking Democrats.

As much as the left loves to hate Sarah Palin, their hatred isn't reserved solely for perky Christian conservative women; it seems to know no bounds when it comes to hating anyone who is even slightly right-leaning.

During the 2012 elections, after tweeting her support for Mitt Romney, actress Stacey Dash found herself in a hailstorm of furious tweeters:

> She's an indoor slave. You know that, sis. RT *@HelloItsBeyonce*: You ready to head back to the fields, jiggaboo? *@REALStaceyDash* —Sherrick W. (@SimplyShers)

> Stacey Dash has probably been thinking that she's a white woman since her "Clueless" days. All the signs were there. —Thighley Cyrus (@_Khalon)[26]

Through the entire maelstrom of hate, Stacey Dash personally answered almost every tweet—good and bad—with grace, class, and humor. If people didn't know who she was before, you'd better believe conservatives are now going to support Stacey Dash's acting career for the rest of her life.

Regarding name-calling, as a former Democrat I unfortunately understand why statists resort to such childishness. Whenever my longtime Republican husband, Mark, and I would get into political debates, there would always come a point in our conversation when a tiny little light would start flashing in my brain: "Wait! That makes sense! Abort! Abort!" If I were to admit he was right on any given point, I knew that perhaps everything else would start falling apart, too. That's when all those Democratic defensive mechanisms—deflecting, subject changing, and ultimately name-calling—kick into high gear.

Perhaps even worse than the name-calling—and one of the most maddening things about the left—is their blatant hypocrisy. On one hand they appear to be humanitarians, tolerant and loving. But on the other hand, if you don't agree with them, Lord help you!

In 2013, *Desperate Housewives* actress Eva Longoria participated in an anti-bullying campaign. She said, "It's time to stop saying mean things or writing mean things about another person and thinking it's okay. It's time to stop humiliating people because they're different."[27]

Of course this is the same Eva Langoria who tweeted:

RT @imnotyuri: @evalongoria I have no idea why any woman/minority can vote for Romney. You have to be stupid to vote for such a racist/misogynistic twat. —Eva Longoria (@EvaLongoria October 17, 2012)[28]

(Ever–Twitter-vigilant Michelle Malkin published Longoria's tweet before the actress could delete it . . .)

Humanitarian Madonna also has a lot to say about bullying and peer pressure: "We talk a lot about the importance of not judging people who are different, not judging people who don't fit into our accepted . . . view of what's cool and what isn't. . . . Think about somebody beating up on you or bullying you for some choice that you've made in your life."[29] Nice. And yet Madonna seemed to forget to follow her own advice when she bullied a crowd about voting for Obama in 2012. During one of her elitist, uber-expensive concerts (because she hates capitalism and money so much), exuding her usual class and grace, she yelled, "Y'all better vote for f**king Obama, OK? For better or for worse, all right? We have a black Muslim in the White House! Now that's some amazing s**t."[30]

Cher declared in her anti-bullying campaign: "Bullying is a trend for everyone. I don't get that trend. Maybe we're a less nice generation. You see it in all these shows . . . there's a lot of things going on. I don't get it but I've seen it."[31] Cher, you should "get it" because you're doing it. During the 2012 elections, Cher tweeted, "If ROMNEY gets elected I don't know if I can breathe same air as Him & his Right Wing Racist Homophobic Women Hating Tea Bagger Masters."[32]

And there it is, in a nutshell: Right Wing Racist Homophobic Women Hating Tea Bagger. The only thing she left out is religion—but I'm sure she has since made up for that oversight.

Some of these progressive "soldiers" aren't so much into name-calling as they are publicly wishing death on their conservative enemies (along with their families). Anti-bullying advocate comedienne Wanda Sykes once said, "I think Rush Limbaugh was the 20th hijacker but he was just so strung out on Oxycontin he missed his flight . . . Rush Limbaugh, I hope the country fails, I hope his kidneys fail, how about that? He needs a good waterboarding, that's what he needs."[33]

And much respected NPR broadcaster Nina Totenberg said about Jesse Helms (and his family): "[I]f there is retributive justice, [Senator Jesse Helms] will get AIDS from a transfusion, or one of his grandchildren will get it."[34]

Of course, this list is endless, as is the hatred that constantly flows from the left for all things conservative. While they proclaim the GOP started the War on Women, they have also declared their own War on Anyone-Who-Disagrees-with-Them-on-Any-Subject.

Come on, celebrities—you can't play both sides of the fence. If you preach against bullying, don't bully—even if you are bullying someone you think of as a "Tea Bagger racist/misogynist twat."

6

SWAPPING SANITY:
LOVING THE UNLOVABLE

by GINA LOUDON

How comes it, that thou art then estranged from thyself?
—WILLIAM SHAKESPEARE, *THE COMEDY OF ERRORS*

I love the opening line in the movie *Bella*: "If you want to make God laugh, tell Him your plans."[1]

God probably deems me "His little comedian" because I am always blurting out my plans, and He must always be laughing as He shows me that I am mistaken.

One year in high school, after a great accomplishment, I decided to thank God by volunteering at a camp for the mentally disabled that summer. As if I could repay God. The joke was on me. My plan to bless God turned into an abundant blessing for me and planted a seed in my heart. Ultimately, my husband, John, and I adopted Samuel. We both had a desire to adopt, but even that didn't go as planned.

John and I told our friends and family that we intended to adopt a special-needs child. One friend asked if I had considered what it would do to our family photographs. A family member said I was being selfish to impose such a thing on our other children. A political enemy said he was sure we were doing it for political purposes.

We continued to pray about our decision. With more than 90 percent of babies with Down syndrome being aborted, we knew God was calling us to be the parents of a child with Down syndrome. We just had to figure out how. We initially looked at finding a distraught mother inquiring about aborting her baby with Down syndrome. I called Planned Parenthoods directly and told them about my desire to help one of these mothers. They never returned my call.

In the meantime, John and I found out we were expecting twin boys. We were thrilled. Then, one month into my pregnancy, I found out I had a subchorionic hemorrhage and ended up miscarrying again. We were devastated.

One day, shortly after losing our twins, John was in session and I was home alone. I called my best friend from high school, who had just lost her husband in a plane accident. I will never forget the words she said to me: "Gina, you have to trust me on this one. God will restore what the locusts have eaten away" (see Joel 2:25).

What?! How could she? I thought she was my friend, but I would have to be an idiot to rest on some idea that God was going to "restore" my twin boys! *That was the most ridiculous, empty promise she could have ever said to me*, I thought.

Well, in only a matter of weeks we were pregnant again. John had decided to run again and was in the middle of the campaign of his life. This, coupled with his work in the Senate, was taking a toll on our little family. It was 2006, and I already had three little ones.

The week of my birthday, John had to go to the capitol to meet with the governor about a pro-life bill he had been trying to pass for years. It was very important to him, to both of us. I planned on joining him, but my perinatologist ordered me to stay home because I had a subchorionic hemorrhage, again. So John made the trek to the capitol alone, and he asked me not to call him during the day because he would be in hard-core negotiations on his bill. "However" he added, "if you have an emergency, call on my cell three times, and I will know it is you and step out to call you."

And of course, that day of all days, the call came that our family had waited for, for more than a decade. There was a baby in Florida who needed parents. He had Down syndrome and several other conditions. He might not live. He was on a feeding tube and was failing to thrive. I asked if we could wait a day or two to answer, because I wanted time to pray about it with John.

"No," said the businesslike voice on the other end of the phone. "There is a real possibility this baby won't make it." She reminded me that he had several congenital illnesses, a heart problem, a lung issue, failure to thrive, and he was on a feeding tube. "If you decide to sign for his adoption, in all likelihood you could be signing a death certificate, but at least he will die with parents."

I hung up and called John three times. He called me back, just as promised. I told him everything and added that I knew it would painful for all of us if we adopted the baby only to watch him die, but I couldn't bear the thought of him dying alone in the big public hospital with no one to even hold him.

He agreed. "Call her back and tell her yes."

"But . . ." I hesitated. Naysayers' voices ran through my brain like a ticker.

"Listen, honey: this is easy," my wise husband said. "If we don't have room in our hearts and in our homes for this baby, then God does not need me in politics. Now, I have to get back in the mansion. Call your mother, put her on the next plane to Florida so she can hold and love that baby, and we will leave day after tomorrow!"

I had never heard him sound so sure of anything . . . ever.

"Oh, and one more thing," he said. "Congratulations; you are the mother of twin boys again!" Whoa. Just like that, God had restored my twin boys. Now all I had to do was fight for their little lives!

We would name one of the boys Robert Brewster after John's relative Robert, and for Elder William Brewster of the *Mayflower*. The other boy we would name Samuel, because he is the child we had prayed for (see 1 Samuel 1:27).

After being on bed rest for weeks due to my subchorionic hemorrhage, I went to the perinatologist to see if I could possibly make a trip to Florida to adopt Samuel. I will never forget the look on the doctor's face when she came into the exam room after my ultrasound. "Dr. Loudon" she said, "I have never seen this, but your hemorrhage has spontaneously dissipated. I can't diagnose you with an SC now. You are free to walk out of here and go straight to Florida to get that baby! Now, GO!"

The agency called to say that due to interstate compact laws, there would be a thirty-day wait to bring Samuel back across the state lines. We were back at a new low. If we did this, we would certainly lose the campaign. That wouldn't be fair to all our volunteers who had campaigned for months. We couldn't just walk. But we sure as heck couldn't abandon that baby. My mother was at the hospital, bonding with him and loving him, and he was improving. We had to go!

On the way to Florida, John called Senator Webster, who had proposed the bill to save Terri Schiavo, the woman who, at her husband's request but against her family's wishes, was ordered by a judge to be killed by starvation due to a diagnosis of "brain death." We had been blessed to minister to the senator during that time, and thought it might be worth a call.

The senator enthusiastically agreed to make some calls on our behalf, to see if he could "move things along." We kept driving in faith, praying, with one baby inside of me, and the other waiting for us in my mother's arms. Within hours, Senator Webster called to say we would be free to take Samuel home, provided his health was okay, within forty-eight hours. Another miracle.

We arrived to find Samuel safe in my mother's arms, pink, happy, and healthy. Not only was he off of the feeding tube; new tests revealed that he was eating, and growing, and thriving! Virtually all of his health issues, including his heart and lung problems, had disappeared. Just like my hemorrhage only days before had disappeared. Just like the thirty-day waiting period had disappeared. Just as God had promised, He was restoring. I will never forget the day the court officer said the words, "Samuel, welcome to your forever family. You may take him home." I still cry when I write those words. Our lives were forever changed.

We brought Samuel home to the waiting arms of his brothers and sisters after only a week. His brother "Bo" was born happy and healthy, and loved him from day one. My plan at that point was to reject those who rejected Samuel. "The people who could reject someone with Down syndrome deserve their own kind of rejection," I reasoned. But God had other plans for that too.

Samuel has taught me grace for the unforgiving, love for the hateful, and hope for the hopeless. Samuel doesn't focus on those who don't love him. He is fixed on the love he sees, and he finds joy in things I could never appreciate before. He taught me to love the unlovable, and I think we in politics have a lot to learn from my Samuel.

My family and I had prayed and planned to fight the culture war in California, because we knew that the real battle for the heart of America was there. We planned for years that when John term-limited out of the Senate, and God gave him a window, we would go. We love the surf and the sea, and we wanted to be on the beach. Many years it seemed totally impossible, even silly to pursue that dream, but we felt it was a calling.

John termed out, and I ran for his seat and lost. It was a hard year, but the political pot was churning, and I was watching as the DC establishment shoved candidate after candidate down the throats of the good old grassroots folks who did most of the work!

I wanted to take down the DC establishment. But how?

John always told me that the real power was in the pen—the media. I knew I wanted to become involved in that. And I wanted to do it in California, so I could write about the culture war and engage on the front lines of the battle.

I started with a little radio show on a station in St. Louis, and soon I syndicated into the flagship superstation of the same company in Alabama. I loved the South faster than a flea jumps when ya flick it. Yet, I was afraid to move there and take over the massive PM Drive slot on the superstation. I was a Yankee-sounding St. Louisan, and I wondered if I would even be accepted in Dixie.

I arrived the day after the horrible tornadoes that killed hundreds swept the South, and all I had to carry me for twenty-four-hour radio coverage was my heart. I knew how to listen and love. Nobody facing that kind of devastation wanted to talk politics. They needed ice, water, shelter, food, medicine, and hope. They needed a voice who was trained for crisis, who could help them find their courage, and who could pray with them. I quickly learned I was born for that moment, and I bonded with my audience in Alabama in deep, deep ways that only a Southerner can understand.

John secured a great job as communications director for the Alabama Senate. We were as happy as hogs in slop!

One night, as we sat over a glass of wine, in our beautiful home at the top of a mountain, we guessed that maybe we weren't called to California to fight the culture wars, after all. We were so happy, so blessed, and we wanted it to last forever. We loved the South, but it was as if God was giving us a respite between political life and what would come.

The next morning, after a night of feeling so content and blessed where we were, John got a call from a headhunter who offered him his dream job. The money was perfect, and it was in beautiful, sunny San Diego. John told the recruiter he was happy where he was and wouldn't be taking the job. I immediately felt convicted and told him to call them back and tell them yes!

My heart broke as I told my Bama audience to "Go boldly, now, and live the truth" one last time, and I knew life would never be that Southern brand of sweet again. It was time for war.

I told God my plans. I know: you would think by now that I would stop that nonsense, but I did it. I would soon learn that my plan of moving to San Diego and quietly taking a local radio spot was not part of His plan. God had far more public things in mind for me, including loving the unbelievably unlovable. If I had known, I might have stayed on my mountain in Alabama.

The very first thing that happened when we got to SoCal was that I stood alongside other doctors and spoke to hundreds of patriots about the problems that would come from Obama's government takeover of our medical system. I told them how pleased I was to be in the heart of Hollywood so I could battle on the front lines of the culture war.

But was I really a warrior? I was about to find out, in painful ways.

A casting director called me the very next day and said he wanted my family to participate in ABC's *Wife Swap*. I told him no. He kept calling. I kept telling him no.

Why would I want to be subjected to being made a fool, or worse? Why would I want to go on one of those stations that only ever tried to make conservatives look bad? Why would I risk a solid career and a happy life for the likes of a network that was critical of all that I do?

Then I was confronted with my own words. What kind of "culture warrior" was I if I didn't even have the courage to battle on enemy turf?

I had done Al Jazeera and Comedy Central's *Daily Show with Jon Stewart*, but *Wife Swap*? That was just plain crazy.

I prayed. I asked my pastor. I talked to my family.

And just as I hadn't planned, my family and I participated in ABC's *Wife Swap*. Those who understood our hearts to communicate with those on the other side were very excited for us to enter the front lines of the battlefield that we have always loved. Others criticized. We expected as much.

Wife Swap isn't what it sounds like. There is no swapping of anything other than a contrived exchange of lifestyles. My family was paired with a polygamous group who forbade any conversation of politics or religion in their house. They wanted us to call their group "polyamorous." They were pro-abortion, pro–"marry whomever and as many whomevers as you like," and there was a lot more yelling and anger than I was used to—at least by the one man in the group. As viewers could see (and he eventually conceded), he was verbally abusive and hateful toward me, even calling my child with special needs horrible things. I felt traumatized from day one.

I demanded to stay in a hotel instead of their duplex when it became clear that my battle was not against flesh and blood but against spiritual forces of evil (Ephesians 6:12). The ABC-affiliated production company forbade me to have my phone, computer, and any other connection with the outside world, with the exception of a one-hour phone meeting with my office to handle only business items. I was not allowed to discuss anything regarding my family.

Given the nature of the show, I had expected to meet a couple with a different dynamic and culture than my own. But I had expected to meet a *couple*. I thought maybe a gay couple or an "Occupy Wall Street" couple, something to contrast my politics. I was excited to surprise America with my ability to love whomever God put in my path.

But I had only considered *couples* who wanted to discuss views of the US Constitution or the Bible or some other religious text. I was game for all of that. But I wasn't at all prepared for multiples (more than two people in a sexual relationship) siding against me and not willing to discuss anything of substance. I was forbidden to talk about religion, history, philosophy, or politics. There was nothing of substance to discuss. And the man of the family berated and ridiculed me without even trying to understand me.

Eleanor Roosevelt diagnosed the problem years ago: "Great minds discuss ideas. Average minds discuss events. Small minds discuss people." And that's just where the conversation usually went at that house—to belittling people. And I was the people.

Whenever I would try to discuss something of substance, the man of the house would be annoyed and fly off the handle. Conversations went something like this:

HIM: You should believe what I believe, and you are mean and narrow-minded if you don't.

ME: Based on what?

HIM: Because you should. Otherwise you are mean and hate filled.

ME: Based on what authority?

HIM: It's obvious.

ME: Well, it isn't obvious to me. Please explain.

HIM: People who believe what you believe are haters. You hate me because of how I live my life.

ME: I do? I don't remember saying that.

HIM: It's obvious. And you're an idiot in denial if you can't see that.

Subsequent conversations left me bewildered and afraid. I would go back to my hotel room again, alone. Without my family or any support, I turned to God for comfort and wisdom.

GOD-SENT FRIENDS

In advance of the show, I had confided in only a couple of very close friends. One of those friends made it her personal mission to run in advance of me and think what would make it "well with my soul," during the difficult circumstances while separated from my family. Angela Love (perfect name) sent me a treasure box full of things to open each day on the show. She even sent extra items just in case the shooting went long.

Initially when I packed my suitcase (on camera, in front of the crew), the network told me that I couldn't bring my treasure box from Angela. I decided I wouldn't go if I couldn't bring it. I didn't know what was in it, but I offered them the opportunity to look through it and remove anything that violated my contract. I was permitted to take it.

Exhausted by the daily isolation from my family and friends, and dealing with the hate and degradation happening on set, I found the little treasures a measure of solace from the dark moments. I would get to my hotel room and see my treasure box and open that day's treasures from my friend with the anticipation of a starving traveler discovering a bountiful feast. Those little joys reminded me that I wasn't dead yet.

There were photos that Angela had downloaded and printed from my Facebook page, knowing I would have no access to social media. She had lovingly enclosed little photos of those I love, smiling and happy, and of my family and friends. She was meticulous. She had inserted small gifts, little things I love: chocolate-covered bacon (my favorite candy bar), inspirational quotes, biblical wisdom, and letters. She even included words about how things would be when I finally got home. As home began to seem farther and farther away, I depended on her "treasures" in more ways than I can describe.

At the hotel, when I had a moment alone, that little treasure box and my Bible were my only companions. I was never told when I would be called, so I would spend hours alone in my sparse hotel room. I wasn't allowed to go anywhere or talk to anyone. I knew nothing about the challenges my family was experiencing. I was utterly in the dark, and I endured this alone. The only conversations I had were with the man whose house I had to shoot in each day, and as the world could later see, most of those were vitriolic and incited.

There was a convention of a Missionary Baptist church in the hotel where I was staying. There were so many sweet-looking ladies walking around. I just wanted to pull one of them into my hotel room and pour my heart out and have one of them hold me. They looked so secure, and so full of love. I needed a hug, a kind word, or just a moment of affection, worse than a drop of water in a dry desert. I was wholly isolated.

COMPLETELY ALONE

Being an only child, I'm used to being alone. But in this age of cell phones, television, multimedia, and social media, most of us rarely, if ever, are utterly alone. I was isolated from everyone and everything except those who sought to discredit me.

Isolation for days on end is so much more agonizing than I knew. My mind went to prisoners of war who were locked in isolation not knowing if they would ever see loved ones again. I had it so easy compared to them. At least I knew an end would come. But as the days became more torturous, the light at the end of the tunnel was harder to see. I became irrational, and I doubted my sanity. I was very lost in my head, if that makes sense. I began to doubt everything I thought I knew, and even began to really care about the success of the show. It became a priority over my own physical or emotional health. I cared more about the show than about being treated with dignity or respect. I was experiencing classic Stockholm syndrome, though I didn't know it at the time. I began to think that maybe I should go along more with things the producers were asking me to do, just to get it all over with so I could go back to my hotel. I was losing it.

One night, after a horrible day of taping in which I was asked to shave the back of the man who had said terrible things about my child, it dawned on me—I wasn't kidnapped. I was still a free person, in a free country, and I could leave.

No one had ever left an episode of *Wife Swap*, and I knew I would be criticized. I also knew that this was *not* what I had bargained for, and that to stay was to risk my mental and physical health. I wanted the message of the show to really reveal my heart (and the compassion of a conservative), and I wanted to love that group of people until they understood me, too. I wanted to find a way to tell the group that I could love them without compromising my convictions. But at a certain point it became obvious that the man in the house wasn't interested in knowing my heart at all. I couldn't change that. While I was alone, he had a spare "wife" with him at night to share with, talk to, and feel affection from. He also had access to Internet and his cell phone, I believe. I abided 100 percent by the rules. I stayed until I realized that I was on the verge of casting pearls before swine (see Matthew 7:6), and compromising far more than I meant to compromise.

During the next abusive conversation, I came to my senses, gathered my things, and walked off the set. I felt I had failed the show, but I knew I'd made the right decision. I agonized over the hell I knew my family had endured all week, and now I was walking away. I felt like a total failure, but ironically, I knew I was doing the right thing.

My reunion with my family and friends after days and days of hell was the sweetest of all time. I had lost almost fifteen pounds off of my five-foot-two frame, and my mind was weak. My husband said I was unrecognizable on the phone or in person.

The actual taping of the episode was the worst experience of my life. I came away traumatized, and yet my analytical mind could not help being amazed at what I saw and felt. I learned so much.

LESSONS IN MADNESS

Through my *Wife Swap* encounter I learned that God uses negative, even horrible experiences to change you and make you stronger, and that it is darkest right before the dawn and the promise of a new day. I also learned that I am a survivor—that my breaking point is beyond what I could have imagined—and I am stronger than I thought. What's more, I have the best friends and support system in the entire world. And there is nothing better in the whole world than the family God chose for me. Through it all, I discovered that I knew how to endure right up to the last endurable moment, and then I knew to cut bait. Most of all, I learned that God carries us through our darkest days, and that the treasures earned in dark times are the sweetest of all.

I came home and battled nightmares and posttraumatic stress, along with other things that I had never experienced in my life. Even so, I was forever changed in ways that some meant for evil, but God meant for good.

UNLIKELY ALLIES

When the show finally aired, months after filming in upstate New York, I was overwhelmed by the response. I fully expected the usual parade of naysayers on both sides to spew their rhetoric. To their side, I was a homophobic hating machine who wanted to hurt women, take away choice, and impose my moral theocracy on this otherwise wonderfully humanistic postmodern world. On my own side, I was a self-glorifying traitor who gave ABC legitimacy, and since no real conservative would ever grace those evil people with their presence, I must have ulterior motives.

A quote by Rick Warren motivated me to say yes to the casting director when he asked if I would be a swapped wife for ABC: "Our culture has accepted two huge lies. The first is that if you disagree with someone's lifestyle, you must fear or hate them. The second is that to love someone means you agree with everything they believe or do. Both are nonsense. You don't have to compromise convictions to be compassionate."[2]

I wanted to demonstrate that to the world.

I thought ABC's portrayal of me and my personality was relatively accurate. I thought their portrayal of my husband was not. John and I had been separated and isolated. The bully on the playground had a convenient ally in his spare wife who was not swapped. That made a huge and fascinating psychological difference, in my subsequent analysis. None of that really matters; what matters to me still is what America thought, or more accurately, did my participation in *Wife Swap* make America think?

The fan mail poured in. The hate mail poured in. I am used to both. Neither really affects me much, because they are part of public life, and I have lived very publicly most of my life.

But this is what was pivotal: One evening soon after the airing of our ABC episode, my producer sent me a copy of a tweet that he thought I should see. It came from a flamboyant entertainer and talk show host named Xander Gibb. My time on *Wife Swap* had had an impact on him. He wrote this as a historic account many months after the airing of *Wife Swap*:

For as long as I can remember I have had [a] healthy interest in politics & was like most of us spoon fed party lines & media hype, from the left & the right, from Republicans & Democrats alike. In my brain Republicans were haters & hated gays & didn't want them to have any rights & only wanted you to see their point of view & party perspective. None were ever willing to sit down & dialogue, preferring to quote party lines & throw spin at me, so I gave up trying. I instead like a sheep followed & questioned not enough.

I love the TV Show The View & would watch Elisabeth Hasselbeck go back & forth with Joy Behar. I always agreed with Joy & began to hate Elisabeth for her Republican perspective on life, yes I said hate! I gradually became ashamed of the fact that I hated someone for their political beliefs, yes me, Xander Gibb the tireless fighter for Equality & Understanding hated a Woman I had never met because she was a Republican.

We are indoctrinated by the media to show disdain for those who disagree with us entirely [and] that never the twain shall meet. My shame made me a little more tolerant of people in general, regardless of their political leanings, even Hasslelbeck. . . .

One night I was watching an episode of Wife Swap . . . Two families swapped the Mom of the house for a week & the families couldn't have been more different. One was a Conservative family & the Mom was a Conservative Talk Show host & Christian, married to a former Missouri Senator. The other was a Polygamist Family with 2 moms who tried to sell their lifestyle as being no different from being gay & that it should be accepted by society.

I really couldn't identify with either family in the beginning & in typical TV fashion, the show was edited in a way that portrayed the Conservative Mom as homophobic. Having worked in television, I should have known better, but gave no thought to the editing process & how it can be used to sculpt comments in an out of context way.

Ever willing to point out any kind of discrimination, I took to the internet & flexed my Social media muscles & promptly attacked the Conservative Mom, undeservedly. I think the comment was something along the lines of "You may dress like a Christian, but that is where the similarity ends."

Anyone else would have blocked me & ignored me but . . . not this Conservative Republican, not Dr. Gina Loudon.

Dr. Gina Loudon was the very first republican that entered into civil discourse with me. She didn't toe the party line, or defend every single thing that the Republicans had ever done. Though highly principled Dr. Gina took the chance over a long period of time to enter into that "Civil Discourse" which quite honestly changed my whole thinking on Republicans. . . .

We have both been criticized by our peers. [I] have even been called a traitor for dialoguing with Republicans as a Democrat. I am no longer a Democrat, so that fixes that & I now choose to call myself a Libertarian.

My political evolution grows & with that my message has evolved too. I question & research every point. Can you imagine the immense difference . . . in this country if we all stopped judging, quoting party lines, apportioning blame & actually began by looking at the things we agree on, the things that unite us? Our love of America should be stronger than our dislike of those who disagree with us Socially or Politically.

I am genuinely convinced & not from any Utopian Ideology . . . that this will bring us all together & unite us in making this great land the greatest once again. America is in trouble & most Politicians will not sell you unity, or joint working or any message of this kind. We need to work together for left & right to effect the urgent change required to get us through these dark times. Let's celebrate that which unites us [and quiet] the political scoffers by becoming true agents of change. God Bless America.[3]

Xander's response to my very public appearance on ABC was heartening. There were hundreds, or maybe thousands, of lower-profile letters that said things like, "After watching you on *Wife Swap*, I realized that I am actually on the side of the haters, and that has changed my life! I watched you respond in love, and you changed my perception of conservatives. Rock on, Dr. G!"

There were so many. Even Rush Limbaugh, Glenn Beck, and

Dr. Gina Loudon before she was devoted to keeping politicians in line

Morgan with Ron Howard in *The Andy Griffith Show* episode "Opie's First Love" (1966)

ABOVE: Morgan with Patrick Duffy in the television show *Dallas. (1983)* Photograph courtesy of Lorimar Productions

LEFT: Morgan with Fred MacMurray in *My Three Sons* (1960)

ABOVE: Ann-Marie's first acting headshot

RIGHT: Ann-Marie in the Miss Texas pageant (1981)

ABOVE: Morgan as Katherine Wentworth in a publicity photo for *Dallas* (1981). Photograph courtesy of CBS

LEFT: Morgan as Vivien Leigh in *Moviola—The Scarlett O'Hara War* (1980)

Ann-Marie with Lt. Col. Allen West (Photograph by Marc Langsam)

Ann-Marie interviewing Congressman Louie Gohmert in 2012 on the steps of the Supreme Court the day they began Obamacare hearings

Ann-Marie interviewing Sen. Pat Toomey in DC

Ann-Marie interviewing Michele Bachmann in 2012

Dr. Gina with Jon Stewart and his three-legged rescue pit bull Dippy (so sweet!) at Comedy Central HQ in NYC

Dr. Gina being interviewed by Greg Gutfeld on *The O'Reilly Factor* on Fox News

Dr. Gina with Bret Baier in the Fox DC studio

Dr. Gina's "game face" just before a hit on Fox News

Dr. Gina at home in the range (Hoover Tactical Firearms in Birmingham, Alabama) showing off the fully automatic FN F2000

Ann-Marie interviewing James Patrick Riley, star/creator of *Courage, New Hampshire*

Morgan with Speaker Tip O'Neill on the Congressional lawn for March of Dimes Walk America

ABOVE: Morgan with Mayor Rudy Guliani during his run for president

RIGHT: Morgan with Speaker Dick Armey and Rep. Buck McKeon at a fundraiser for Rep. Buck McKeon (They were trying to convince me to run for office!)

Ann-Marie, Morgan, and Dr. Gina enjoying a casual outtake at the Reagan Library

Sean Hannity discussed the show and completely got it. But more important to me than the fan mail or attagirls by my colleagues and mentors, were the powerful letters of conversion and transformation that happened to regular, everyday people who saw in that show something different that changed their perspective forever. The show was a lightbulb of sorts, and the letters from people who "see the light" continue to this day as the show re-airs on various networks.

Staff and volunteers went through all of my mail, e-mail, instant messages, and other correspondence to be sure I got to read all of the best ones. And I knew right then exactly why I had traveled the journey I had. And I felt thankful.

To this day I am not sure there is a deeper pleasure than to feel used by God for His purpose. Though my little part is only minis-cule, I still feel honored every time I get another letter of conversion, and I still get them from that show. Not for self-righteous reasons at all. I am still a student of this world, with a ton to learn. But mostly I am thankful just to have been a part of something that really helped people see people instead of labels.

A REASON TO BELIEVE

All of these lessons I have learned still leave me with a question: What is it about some people that they just can't have a rational conversation with someone with whom they disagree? How is it that so many of us are so manipulated to believe that all of those on the other side are evil?

I submit that the great divide doesn't really exist between rank-and-file Republicans and Democrats, or even union versus open-shop dissenters, or between big-government advocates and small-government advocates. I think that the power elite in Wash-ington would like for us to believe that, but I don't think it is so. I believe that not only do the DC elite create and narrate the real problems in this world, but they also promulgate them to maintain their power.

The sobering reality is that we the people are still the hoi polloi. We don't have K Street or Wall Street to fund our efforts. We don't control the IRS, TSA, SEC, or NSA and use them to harass our enemies. This might require a revolution, of sorts. But, ah, the vindication. Can we just enjoy that for a moment? We knew we weren't crazy, but now they have to at least wonder if maybe we weren't onto something all along.

They were told that we were rich and evil. If we were never the rich ones, that only leaves evil. But if we aren't warmongers and genuinely do care about the poor and the well-being of our fellow citizens, how evil can we really be?

Once we find common ground, there is an opportunity to talk. I am not saying we should, for a moment, compromise who we are or what we believe. In fact, I hate the word *compromise*—that is what establishment Republicans do. That is not going to get anyone anywhere in today's conflict. I am saying simply to engage.

On my show I jest that we should "find a liberal to love." I mean it, mostly. So far, though, the timing has been bad, because the odium has been too deep.

Jonathan Haidt wrote a brilliant book called *The Righteous Mind.*[4] I like this book because Haidt attempts to explain the philosophical divide between liberals and conservatives. He spells out the differences between what is morally sacred on the right and on the left. He also explains moral motivators that cause political polarization and enmity. Haidt suggests that there are moments and approaches that may help us work together, at least on the big issues, like jobs and economy. I would say our country is in one of those moments now.

Dr. Haidt contends that the sacred morality of modern liberalism is that they care. That doesn't mean conservatives don't care, and he details that also. But liberals disproportionately care about the oppressed compared to other issues in the world or passions they might have. They also care who cares. They perceive that conservatives don't care, at least not as much as we should, about certain oppressed groups.

Conservatives, in turn, get annoyed at being told they don't care, because they do. Conservatives also get very annoyed that the liberals seem to care more than think, and therefore, they react emotionally to what the conservatives deem a problem easily solved through intellect.

Dr. Haidt worked with Brian Nosek and Jesse Graham to create a site called YourMorals.org. They developed a matrix based on questions asked about how people value certain aspects of six moral foundations: care, liberty, fairness, loyalty, authority, and sanctity.

The graph shows that those who label themselves "liberal" value care, liberty, and fairness disproportionately, and much more than the other three foundations. Those who label themselves politically conservative tend to value all six foundations more equally.

Though Dr. Haidt respects the balance and even the ideas of the self-labeled conservative, he believes, as I do, that the elite in the Republican Party today are not consistent with the values of

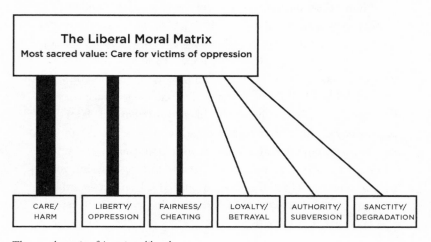

The moral matrix of American liberal.

the rank-in-file conservative. He goes so far as to call GOP leaders today "a curse upon the land."[5] He believes the leadership of the party has gone astray, and the elite in both parties are detached from the grass roots. Despite being an admitted Democrat, Dr. Haidt is an outspoken critic of the Obama administration.

His idea, initially, was to help liberals understand the mind of the conservative. His work has led to dialogue on both sides, and a shift in vitriol at leaders behaving badly.

The differences among those who lead and those who believe in the two ideologies are vast.

As I've pointed out, the liberals' strong desire to help others clouds their judgment on the best way to do that. They may want to help their child do well in school, but if they do the child's work for him and never let him fail, they are hurting rather than helping. Likewise, the liberals want to help the poor, but if they provide free housing and food through government subsidies, they will eventually ruin the economy for everyone and destroy the opportunity for the poor to ever better themselves. Here is a simple economic example of how that works:

Markets Are Miraculous. . . .
Now let's do the devil's work and spread chaos throughout the marketplace. Suppose that one day all prices are removed from all products in the supermarket. All labels too, beyond a simple description of the contents, so you can't compare products from different companies. You just take whatever you want, as much as you want, and you bring it up to the register. The checkout clerk scans in your food insurance card and helps you fill out your itemized claim. You pay a flat fee of $10 and go home with your groceries. A month later you get a bill informing you that your food insurance company will pay the supermarket for most of the remaining cost, but you'll have to send in a check for an additional $15. It might sound like a bargain to get a cartload of food for $25, but you're really paying

your grocery bill every month when you fork over $2,000 for your food insurance premium.

Under such a system, there is little incentive for anyone to find innovative ways to reduce the cost of food or increase its quality. The supermarkets get paid by the insurers, and the insurers get their premiums from you. The cost of food insurance begins to rise as supermarkets stock only the foods that net them the highest insurance payments, not the foods that deliver value to you.

As the cost of food insurance rises, many people can no longer afford it. Liberals (motivated by Care) push for a new government program to buy food insurance for the poor and the elderly. But once the government becomes the major purchaser of food, then success in the supermarket and food insurance industries depends primarily on maximizing yield from government payouts. Before you know it, that can of peas costs the government $30, and all of us are paying 25 percent of our paychecks in taxes just to cover the cost of buying groceries for each other at hugely inflated costs.[6]

It has been proven that when you subsidize something, you get more of it. If you want to end poverty, don't subsidize it. Likewise, if you don't have to pay for things, the quality will diminish and the price will skyrocket. It is astonishing to me how the liberals "embrace Darwin and reject 'intelligent design'" when explaining the natural world. But they embrace an intelligent designer (government policy) and reject "Adam Smith as an explanation for design and adaptation in the economic world."[7]

Based upon this logic, we would be best to avoid morality with liberals, because our sacred matrices are too different. Instead, Dr. Haidt says, find what you agree on (perhaps the attack on Syria, or the arrogance of the political class in DC), and prove yourself compassionate and human. (They have been told you are neither.) Then you have something to build upon.

So after you have your "vindication celebration," stop and take a look at where we are in our history. Invite someone you think is unlovable to dinner to talk about the unspeakable—politics and religion. The enemy is quickly becoming "They the Imperial." That gives "We the People" so much to confabulate. This might just be our miracle moment.

The enemy may not be who we thought it was. It might be the unlovable, even if that wasn't our plan.

PART 3

WHAT WOMEN *REALLY* WANT

7

CREATING AN ARMY OF WOMEN FROM SCRATCH

by ANN-MARIE MURRELL

I volunteered to fight in this war. I have risen through the ranks and now find
myself on the front lines with an army of New Media warriors following me into
the fray. It is no longer a choice to fight; I am compelled to fight.[1]

—ANDREW BREITBART

After my 9/11 conversion experience and my *Liberty and Tyranny* eye-opener (see chapter 1), I began to really pay attention to what was happening to my country and the world. It was then that the things that were really important to me began to take shape. It wasn't so much about lattes and Hollywood gossip with friends as it was about whether propositions and Senate bills would pass. I knew that what women really want is to be empowered to make a difference in the world beyond the trivial things. So I became a political activist.

I got my first break writing for Red White Blue News and quickly began contributing to other news sites, like Liberty Alliance, which is a network of websites dedicated to advancing life, liberty, and the pursuit of happiness. It wasn't long into my political reporting career that the prospect of being in front of the camera came up again. When I left show business in the mid-1990s, I was surprised at how much happier I became. For most of my life I had been involved in some form of show business, from my child-hood watching both of my parents rehearse plays to my mostly bit-part acting days in Hollywood. While I passionately loved the actual "show" part, I hated the "business" part. I dreaded auditions, constantly putting my heart and soul out there for someone else to judge and, more often than not, dealing with rejection. Even in my best years, when I had the "youth and beauty" thing going for me, I was told I was too everything: too young, too old, too tall, too short, too perky, too pretty, too *whatever*. When I was in my early twenties, an agent even encouraged me to have plastic surgery to shave off part of my "too pointy" chin. (I refused. I like my chin.)

So when Atlanta website magnates at Liberty Alliance asked me to do a video show for their website Patriot Update (where I had been a columnist for a few years), I initially declined. I was thrilled with the prospect of aging gracefully and never having to worry about being in front of the camera again. The thought of dieting and fretting over lines and wrinkles made me a little ill. But they persisted and ultimately talked me into doing a weekly series of videos for their site. I was surprised that without anyone on earth knowing who I was, the *Patriot Update with Ann-Marie Murrell* ended up garnering a few thousand fans (many who are still with me today on Facebook and Twitter).

From there, I took my camera and microphone on the road and started covering conservative political events all over California. Back then, no one was doing that; I was the only person asking people like Larry Elder, AlfonZo Rachel, and other conservative pundits and authors for on-camera interviews. Each time I went to an event, I thought, *Certainly other people will catch on, and I'll have to compete for camera time*, but it never happened. (Even today, I'm often one of the only reporters covering conservative events and doing on-camera interviews.)

At the same time I was doing my Patriot Update reporting, *Saturday Night Live* actress-comedienne Victoria Jackson was doing her own series of videos and reports for Liberty Alliance. Victoria and I met at comedienne-writer Sonya Schmidt's house for an interview one day, and that is what I think caused the wheels to start rolling at Liberty Alliance.

"What would you think about the possibility of doing a conservative talk show, featuring you and Vicki?" Brandon Vallorani asked me on the phone one day. "We're thinking it would be sort of the conservative alternative to *The View*."

Without even pausing, I said yes. For the next few months, we exchanged dozens of e-mails and had multiple phone conversations formulating plans and ideas about the show.

In addition to Victoria and me, two other cast members were chosen: my Patriot Update editor, Jenny Jones, and one of Victoria's friends, pro-life advocate Jannique Stewart.

One day, as we were talking about possible names for the show, Jenny said, "One of the names we're thinking of is Liberty Gals." I hated it. I immediately heard the song "Buffalo Gals" in my head and pictured old-fashioned women wearing June Cleaver dresses with sparklers coming off their heads.

Jenny agreed with me, and then said, "We also thought of the name PolitiChicks."

If I remember correctly, my initial reaction was to scream, "That's IT!" It was the perfect name: a play on the word *politics* and also a very un–politically correct, cheeky name for a woman. We were all sick to death of any and all forms of PC, and the people who told us not to call women "chicks" were the same feminazi types who told women to burn their bras and let it all hang out in the sixties.

Thus the *PolitiChicks* web TV show was born.

From there things happened pretty fast. Liberty Alliance had a studio in their Atlanta offices where they filmed a few small video shows, so Vicki, Jannique, and I flew from our respective states to Atlanta. Each month, we would film four to six episodes at a time. We didn't really have any set plans other than deciding on a few topics and agreeing that Victoria would play her ukulele and maybe throw in a song or two. Because of Victoria's fame, we garnered a lot of attention from the left. A lot—and much of it not very nice.

HUFFINGTON POST: Victoria Jackson's 'PolitiChicks': Former 'SNL' Star Launches Anti-Gay, Anti-Muslim Web Show[2]

GAWKER: *PolitiChicks* is a Conservative Version of *The View* from Hell[3]

PEREZ HILTON: The show aims to be weekly, and you can think of it as *The View* but with a deep seeded foundation in ultraconservatism.[4]

MEDIAITE: Is it supposed to be funny and light-hearted? Sort of a *Daily Show* for conservatives, or *The Five* for women? Is it supposed to be like a talk show, something akin to *The View* sans Barbara, Joy or Whoopi? Or is it supposed to be a more serious, nuanced look at today's headlines? Because it seems to me that Jackson is on a completely different show from the other three ladies, with her own, completely different hair stylist.[5]

Each of us got attacked verbally for just about everything, from our views and opinions to the way we look. "In the video, the bags beneath Ann's eyes droop lower than Rodney Dangerfield's self-esteem," wrote one especially snarky blogger. Meh. Luckily, all my years in show business, being harshly judged and criticized for my looks, made me much stronger, and comments like that don't bother me anymore. I figure at my age, if a woman doesn't have bags under her eyes, she's either a freak of nature or she's had plastic surgery.

The following month we left the "green wall" and moved our show into Luke and Jo Anne Livingston's Ground Floor Video studios in Woodstock, Georgia. I introduced Liberty Alliance to my friend, movie producer Beverly Zaslow (of *Runaway Slave* and *Hating Breitbart* fame), and between Beverly and Luke our show became crisp, fun, and light-years more professional. We had some amazingly great guests: Frank Gaffney, Bill Whittle, AlfonZo Rachel, Fred Grandy, and more. Because of Beverly (and Luke), I was able to snag some incredible interviews, including Congresswoman Michele Bachmann in her Washington, DC, office; Frank Gaffney in the Heritage Foundation building; and probably the most important interview of my life, Andrew Breitbart at his final CPAC.

There were a few things we didn't like about the show, mainly the tall stools. We hated them, in fact. And we didn't like saying, "PolitiChicks" all together in the intro. Otherwise, it was a blast.

From inception to the spring of 2012, our cast members came and went. Victoria moved on to create her own web series, *The Victoria Jackson Show*. Morgan Brittany, who had been a guest on our show, became a cast member, followed by Dr. Gina Loudon and Breitbart heroine Sonnie Johnson. PolitiChicks was finally complete—and then, for multiple reasons (mainly logistics), in May 2012 Liberty Alliance decided they weren't going to do a studio show anymore. Instead, they asked me if I would take over the PolitiChicks website and create a brand-new PolitiChicks 2.0. Liberty Alliance had previously asked me to be the national director and editor in chief of PolitiChicks, but because of the demands of filming, I didn't have time. I knew we still had this amazing thing, and I didn't want it to disappear, so for the next month, I created a binder full of plans. I asked for assurance that I would have full creative control, and the ability to change PolitiChicks into more of a serious and relevant—yet still fun—website. Liberty Alliance said "absolutely." So in June 2012, I flew to Atlanta to help redesign PolitiChicks.tv.

POLITICHICKS NATIONWIDE

The giant red lips were the first thing to go. The lips made up our previous logo, studio set, and PolitiChicks T-shirts. Yes, it was cute, but I felt the name *PolitiChicks* said it all. We're already all about red lips, big hair, makeup, and femininity—no need to slug people in the face with it. So good-bye, lips; hello, "Rosie the Riveter"–style logo—much more representative of today's conservative woman. I also substituted all the pastel colors on the site for bold, unapologetic red, white, and blue. My overall goal, which I believe our design team achieved, was to create a site that was as clean and uncomplicated as possible.

And then there were my anchors and the women I considered to be the heart of PolitiChicks, my cast mates, Morgan, Gina, and Sonnie. Although we weren't going to have a studio show anymore, the four of us were such a dynamic team I wanted to find a way to keep us together. Sonnie had other contractual obligations with Breitbart, but Morgan and Gina agreed to hang on—despite the fact that none of us really knew what was going to happen.

After establishing our PolitiChicks anchors, the biggest change I wanted to make—and by far my biggest challenge—was to gather a team of writers from across the United States and create a new movement of conservative activists.

Sarah Palin was absolutely right when she talked about "mama grizzlies." When women feel that their family or their home is under attack, you'd better believe they'll take action. Just like in

1979, when a drunk driver killed Beckie Brown's son. She took action and formed a group of mothers who wanted to protect their children against drunk drivers. That's the exact maternal feeling so many conservative women had in that they felt they were needed to help save our country.

So I started searching social media for my new team of Politi-Chicks writers. I perused Facebook and Twitter and blogs for women who were passionate about conservatism and had a broad knowledge of politics. Some of my writers had never written for anyone publicly, so we all experienced growing pains together in the beginning. But on September 12, 2012, it finally happened; the new PolitiChicks.tv launched.

Since then, hundreds of writers have come and gone, many to write for other organizations or to launch their own websites. But as far as I'm concerned, once you're a PolitiChick, you're always a PolitiChick.[6]

Today, many of our Nationwide PolitiChicks are being interviewed on radio and television, and they speak at rallies across the United States. One PolitiChick article (written by Oregon PolitiChick and Common Core expert Macey France) was debated in a panel on Al Jazeera TV and nominated for a blogger award at CPAC 2014. While we still have lots of haters, which goes with the territory, we have also gained a new level of respect among our blogger colleagues and peers. In 2013 PolitiChicks.tv was one of the nominees for People's Choice Blogger of the Year, coming in second behind our PolitiDude freedom-fighter friend Robert Spencer's *Jihad Watch*. (If we have to lose, wow—what a great way to go!) Beverly Zaslow, our brilliant studio show producer, continues to support us behind the scenes. Because of Beverly, PolitiChicks.tv/Liberty Alliance has partnered with best-selling author and syndicated radio host Dennis Prager to help promote their Prager University video series.

As for Morgan, Gina, and me, our latest project together is participating in PolitiChicks panels, town hall–type forums in which we get to talk to and answer questions from the audience. We love being able to meet the people who read our articles and share our site, and we especially appreciate the ability to encourage other women—and men—to get involved and become conservative activists in their communities. The three of us speak individually (and together) at events and rallies and on radio and TV shows across the nation, but of course, because we are PolitiChicks, our priorities remain firmly grounded when it comes to God, family, and country (in that order, with a little Second Amendment thrown in for good measure).

It's amazing to see how far we've come from a green-walled web TV show to a full-scale national movement of incredibly awe-inspiring, intelligent, and informed PolitiChicks and PolitiDudes.

HOW TO COMBAT THE SLINGS AND ARROWS OF HATERS

On March 1, 2012, I was in Turks and Caicos on vacation when I got the news that Andrew Breitbart had died. It was so devastating and such important news that I took time from my vacation to broadcast a special message to our PolitiChicks viewers. Here is part of what I said:

> All day I'm looking at shades of aqua and blinding white sand but all I know is that Andrew Breitbart is dead and the world is not as good as it was a day ago.
>
> It feels like one of our Generals in this war against the mainstream media has died.
>
> Andrew Breitbart is one of the reasons I write articles and work on a show like PolitiChicks. He coined the term "Citizen Journalist" to describe this new type of work—which [is] basically . . . going out into our now crazy America and trying to find truth among the

garbage that the mainstream media has forced upon us.

Andrew Breitbart showed us that the statist Monster Machine we're so afraid of is simply a giant balloon—all filled with hot air and bluster and blunder and lies—and that all we have to do is take [a] tiny little pin and poke it to make it all go away.

Andrew Breitbart never avoided confrontation—he *sought it out*. He would walk into groups of angry statist mobs and he would talk to them. He *talked to them*. He would ask protesting union workers simple questions like, "Why are you here?" and "Who paid for your trip?" and they wouldn't know what to say. He proved over and over that all these monsters were made of smoke and mirrors.

Andrew Breitbart paved the way for every one of us to be Citizen Journalists. He made sure that all of us regular Conservatives . . . felt competent enough to fight the force that is the mainstream media. He wrote his book *Righteous Indignation* to remind us that we each needed to feel confident enough to *speak out* when we saw something wrong. He encouraged us to blog and write articles and make videos when we knew something wasn't being told correctly. He told every one of us to *stand strong* when we knew we were being treated badly in a "politically correct" world where our values and principles were taking a back seat to the statist agenda.

Andrew Breitbart taught me that I could say and do whatever I needed—*as long as I was correct in what I was reporting*. If I knew in my heart and mind I was doing the right thing it would only take my God to make me stop.

I will never stop.

I will never be silenced.

I will not allow the mainstream media to be the only voice in America.

Andrew Breitbart said we have to create a "new dialogue" in the mainstream media.

We will continue what he started. I know I will and I hope and pray you will, too.

Rest in peace, Warrior Breitbart. Our war has only started; I am prepared to die for what I believe in. God bless you, my friend.[7]

Like so many conservative bloggers today, when I'm confronted with something frightening, such as shining the light on a truth that people might not want to see, I think of Andrew Breitbart. One of my all-time favorite moments in an interview occurred with Andrew at CPAC 2012. I offhandedly mentioned something about what a hero he is and that he's one of the reasons I got into blogging and reporting. There was a brief moment where Andrew genuinely looked surprised and grateful. I didn't see his reaction until after the video was published, just a few weeks before he died. It meant a lot to me.

It was so much easier being part of the silent majority. As new activists, we've all lost statist friends who were shocked when we started talking back. Before, we laughed it off or tried to change the subject when they denigrated Republicans; now we don't laugh anymore. It's not funny.

Every blogger has a different approach in dealing with haters. Some relish the debate and love to argue with every troll. They think it's fun. They call them out, post their comments all over social media, and challenge others to join the fight. Each of my PolitiChicks writers handles critics differently.

These days when I write or do any type of media, I imagine myself donning a suit of "Breitbart armor." To use a Texas analogy, I put on all my protective gear and just run with that ball as hard and fast as I can. If I get knocked around a bit, so be it. I believe in what I'm doing, and frankly, I don't care what the haters think. Haters hate. If they want to stop hating, fine—I'll be there when they figure it out someday. Until then, I've got to keep going forward.

It's also easy to keep going because of my foundation. My parents are some of the strongest, most courageous people I know, and they raised me in the church with a strong, unwavering faith in God. My stepfather, retired chief petty officer Gene Paul Brown, has inspired me throughout my life. Although he never experienced combat in his twenty years in the military, he did have to overcome some major obstacles in his life. When his parents divorced in the 1940s (rare in those days), he had to help raise his brothers while his mother worked cleaning houses. He left school in the seventh grade so he could take care of his six-year-old and infant brothers. He also worked dozens of odd jobs that included setting pins in a bowling alley, working in grocery stores, and pitching tents for a carnival. After struggling several years to survive, at age seventeen he enlisted in the Navy.

Despite all of his hardships, I have never heard my father complain or sound resentful about his childhood. "Why would I?" he tells me. "That's just life. We were never promised it would be easy or fair. You just do what you have to do and get on with it.

"I believe America is a place to fight for, and it has never let me down. As I retired, after twenty years, I am proud of my service," he says.

My mother, Lou Ellen Brown, grew up dirt-poor in the West Texas oil fields where her father worked as an oil well mechanic. Her mother taught in a one-room schoolhouse, and then my mom ended up teaching high school for almost forty-four years. Mrs. Brown was the type of teacher that would stand on top of her desk to get everyone's attention, or throw chalk at a kid who wouldn't stop talking—and every student loved her and thought of her as their favorite teacher, myself included. If there was a fist (or knife) fight in the hallway, my five-foot-four mother was the teacher who would inevitably break it up, despite the fact that coaches might be standing nearby, watching. And at home, if a bed of copperhead snakes dares to take residence in my parents' yard, if Dad isn't around to kill it, my mother will do it herself. With a garden hoe, if their .22 isn't handy. I come from strong stock.

My parents are the reasons I have discipline, strong principles, and such a deep love and respect for my country.

What all of us activist-blogger types are doing here on the home front is the easy part, of course. Despite a bit of traveling, most of my "fighting" is done in the safety and comfort of my home. Others are out there literally risking their lives—right this moment—for our country. The very least we can all do is make sure our military men and women aren't doing this in vain.

If all we have to do to help save our country is speak up, stand up for what's right, and vote, how in the world can we not do that?

Because of our military's example of true sacrifice, I will never complain about defending my country in every way I possibly can here on the home front—and I'll never take for granted that someone else will take care of it for me in the field. I hope you feel the same, because it's going to take all of us to make this happen.

WHAT YOU CAN DO TO MAKE A DIFFERENCE

As I mentioned at the beginning of this chapter, conservative women really want to be involved and part of making the world a better place for others, and mainly for their children and grandchildren. It's not enough to just sit back and complain.

Almost every day I get asked by conservatives across the United States what they can do to make a difference. The old days of just showing up during election time to canvass neighborhoods, answer at phone banks, or donate money to the RNC simply isn't enough anymore. So many conservatives are finally starting to realize that we are in dire times that require immediate action—but where do you start? How do you go from being a passive member of the silent majority to becoming something many GOP types once considered appalling: activists?

Begin by determining what you can do instead of what you can't.

START A BLOG OR WRITE LETTERS. If you enjoy writing, create a blog (WordPress.com has free websites that are very easy to manage). Or on a simpler basis, if you read or see something you disagree with strongly, write letters to editors and politicians who aren't doing their jobs. Don't assume everyone else is doing this; one of the reasons our politicians lost touch with reality is because we the people lost touch with them.

MAKE PHONE CALLS. If you like talking on the phone, start a weekly regimen of calling any and all politicians who are making a difference—both good and bad. If you hear of a senator or a representative who voted against our Second Amendment, again, don't assume people are going to directly call his or her office in DC. Although thousands may rant and rave on Facebook and Twitter, most people won't call the elected official's office. Yours may be one of the only actual voices that member of Congress hears opposing his or her views, and you just never know when it might make a difference.

TALK TO FRIENDS AND FAMILY. The days of never talking religion and politics in public are over. It's time to speak freely and openly about our beliefs, just as the left has done continually from the start. Don't be afraid to bring up an important subject with your family and friends, especially when it involves something that will ultimately affect both sides of the aisle. You never know who's listening to you, and in some cases it may be the first time someone has even heard the other side of the story. My mom always said, "If I can get through to only one student per year, I feel like a success. Any more than that, and I'm victorious."

The good news is that on a daily basis I'm seeing indications that there are more DINOs (Democrats In Name Only) in the Democratic Party than you might think. There are Democrats out there who disapprove of this steamrolling progressive agenda, and they don't want any part of it. I first noticed this just before the 2012 elections when my Democrat hairdresser asked me, "So how's that president working out for you?"

My hackles immediately went up as they always do when he mentions politics. "He is not working out for me in any way."

Then, for the first time in twenty-plus years of being friends with him, my longtime Democrat hairdresser friend said, "I get the feeling he's trying to hurt America on purpose."

After the initial blast of the "Hallelujah" chorus stopped playing in my head, I calmly said, "Yes, my friend, I believe you're right."

We left it at that—for now.

TALK TO YOUR PASTOR ABOUT POLITICS. It's important these days to find out exactly where your pastor stands regarding the new so-called social justice. For decades the left has been manipulating words like *compassion* and *tolerance* and turning them into weapons they can wield against the church. Even atheists—and strangely, Islamists—have gleefully gotten into the battle against the church, telling them what they can and can't do or say, and to the horror of many conservatives, they are caving.

Have open, honest conversations with your pastor. Maybe gather a group of like-minded church members to approach your pastor and ask about his stance on all the important issues that ultimately affect the church, including abortion and marriage. Help him realize that you will all support him in making strong stances against creeping progressivism. Be strong and tell him if he turns his back on the Bible, you will have to turn your back on him. These are strong words, but just like a powerful politician, a pastor has strong influence on entire communities. In both religion and politics, we can no longer afford unlimited power and influence to go unchecked.

WORK ON ELECTIONS THE MOMENT AN ELECTION IS OVER. That's what Democrats do. They are always in constant election mode, always planning and plotting the next one. Just showing up to vote doesn't cut it anymore, nor does working a few weeks a year helping a campaign. Like it or not, this has got to be a year-round thing. Otherwise, please, oh, please, don't complain when we're suddenly "stuck" with a presidential candidate no one seems to want. The way to ensure that doesn't happen is to remain ever vigilant regarding all local, state, and national elections.

REPORT ANY AND ALL SUSPICIONS OF VOTER FRAUD. In your town, have you heard of any type of voter fraud? Don't assume anyone followed up on it, because chances are, no one did. Catherine Engelbrecht created the organization True the Vote (truethevote. org) to help combat voter fraud across the United States. (Because of this the IRS repeatedly audited Engelbrecht and her family, but that's another story.) Sadly, other than activist James O'Keefe's excellent work with Project Veritas, Engelbrecht is one of the lone voices in America constantly trying to oust the bad votes. Voter fraud is another instance where conservatives initially make a fuss throughout social media, but a few weeks after elections, they become the silent majority again. If you're gifted at making a fuss, please do so when it comes to any suspicions you might have regarding fraudulent elections.

Remember, Saul Alinsky and others like him successfully trained statists on how to manipulate and bully people into submission. It's what they count on. When I was in college, I had a very calculating boyfriend who knew how to push every button in order to make me feel angry, sad, insecure, or all of the above. It was almost as if the only way he felt good about himself was by bringing me down. One day in the middle of one of his rants, a light came on somewhere deep inside of me. I said, "I see what you're doing, and you can't do it anymore!"

It was as simple as that, and I remember the look on his face at having been stripped of his powers. His eyes didn't look as dreamy as they once did; he wasn't quite as tall anymore. When I left him, I became a stronger person and have never looked back.

Statists are very much like that manipulative ex-boyfriend. They will call us names, ridicule us, poke us, prod us, instigate us. There's no purpose to their insults other than to try to elevate themselves and lower all of us—and to try to win approval from the unknowing public.

The buttons the statists have been steadily (and stealthily) pushing for years are finally being challenged. And all good people who truly care about America will eventually start saying, "I see what you're doing now, and you can't do it anymore."

Let's get out there and actively use our gifts and talents to save our country. If not us, who will?

PLATFORMS AND STILETTOS

by GINA LOUDON

She shoots in stilettos; barefoot on the beach. Fearless. . . .
—FROM GINA'S PINTEREST HEADER

When I meet people who don't know me and do not understand my politics, I often begin the conversation by saying, "I am a conservative, but I publicly criticize Karl Rove more than Barack Obama, and John McCain more than Hillary Clinton."

It is important that true conservatives—those who agree that conservatism is a superior ideology to socialism or communism—don't whitewash the Republican Party. I have been in politics for more than twenty years; for fourteen of those I was on the inside as the wife of a Missouri state senator. While I emphatically disagree with the ideas of the Democrat Party, I emphatically abhor those on the conservative side who are part of the problem.

When I moved from St. Louis to Alabama, I remember the bliss of not really knowing the political players in the GOP. I had a sense of dread when I considered that one day, I would start to know who were really the selfless, tireless patriots, and who was using the party and making everyone else look bad.

WHAT'S WRONG WITH THE GOP?

The reality is that there are some really evil people in the world, and some of them are in the Republican Party. It makes me almost ashamed at times to call myself a Republican. I guess it is the nature of the occupation. Politicians have power, and power corrupts. Those who are in politics solely to increase their power are so narcissistic that in many cases they rise up quickly within the conservative movement out of sheer selfish ambition. They rule by intimidation, bullying, and threats, and most around them don't know the truth until they have had their heads stepped on. The good news is that they fall harder than they rose, but in the meantime they make the rest of us look bad.

I have always given my allegiance to the Republican Party, but when the self-absorbed political consultants try to force their establishment, big-government candidates down our throats, it makes me pause. It almost makes me want to vote for a third party. However, the two-party system is very hard to beat. I've studied the issue extensively and concluded that winning with a third party would require a total revolution, not just a popular candidate or a rebellion against the status quo. History shows that minority third parties don't win; they only draw votes from the nearest ideological party. For example, the Socialist Party draws votes from the Democrats, and the Libertarian Party costs votes for the Republicans. Ultimately, third parties are tools used by the major parties against each other.

Just to be clear, I can no longer say that I will always vote Republican. I am always watching to see how arrogant the Republican elite become in the next election. Barring a third-party revolution, the GOP will have my vote. However, I will fight tooth and nail for the planks in the platform and for control of that platform by the grass roots.

Regardless of the party you choose, you should read and know their platform. It is the only real power individuals have over the candidates they elect.

THE POWER OF A PERSON: THE CASE FOR THE PARTY PLATFORM

Grassroots activists know that the only power they have over a candidate once he or she is elected is that individual's loyalty to the party platform. The party platform is the grass roots' contract with their elected officials. The platform establishes a party from the grass roots up rather than having the power trickle down from the elected officials.

How can we accomplish that? How can we get candidates to commit to being accountable to the platform once elected? The answer is more public accountability!

Recently, Missouri Wonk, a research and analysis organization in Missouri, analyzed all the state legislators. (This could be done in any state, and would be a tremendous tool to hold elected officials accountable to the grass roots and their party platform!) My husband has the distinction of being ranked the most conservative (truest to his party's platform) in the State of Missouri Senate.[1] When this report came out, other representatives and senators took note, and it became a bit of a competition. This project needs to happen in every state. It's a wonderful way to hold the elected officials accountable by measuring their records and publicizing the results. It could change the face of politics, most literally!

Some might argue that platforms are passé, that it is old-fashioned to be ideological, because culture is evolving so quickly.

But the wise political consumer knows this argument is made by those who want to distract us from the stealth power grabbers, the Washington elite, who are out to rob us of our rights as protected in our Constitution. In 2011 *Time* magazine asked this question about our great founding document, right on the cover: "Does It Still Matter?" According to the cover story, the Framers of our Constitution couldn't have known about modern-day events, such as the advance in technology, globalism, or even current economic and cultural problems; therefore, says the writer, "we cannot let the Constitution become an obstacle to the U.S.'s moving into the future with a sensible health care system, a globalized economy, an evolving sense of civil and political rights."[2]

Thomas Sowell responded in his June 2011 column: "Most people have enough common sense to know that a constitution does not exist to micro-manage particular 'events' or express opinions about the passing scene. A constitution exists to create a framework for government—and the Constitution of the United States tries to keep the government inside that framework." He continued, "Does the Constitution matter? If it doesn't, then your freedom doesn't matter."[3]

Of course the Constitution matters, and of course our freedoms matter. It is troubling to me when the same political pundits who praise the power of the grass roots and the Constitution try to eliminate the voice of the grass roots by ignoring the party platform. The power of the citizen is gone when the elitists within the parties decide that they can overlook party platforms and make up the rules that they like.

Phyllis Schlafly of Eagle Forum describes the party platform as an essential "creed." It is the symbol of "what we think is worth our work and sacrifice," and the "standard to which public officials may be held accountable."[4]

To understand the critical nature of the party platform, it helps to know the history. Elitists in both national parties prefer that citizens remain naive about the power they wield, so they won't be held accountable and can continue to ram their own candidates through the system.

As Churchill warned, "those who don't learn from history are doomed to repeat it."

In 1992 the Republican National Convention was in Houston. I was there, and I worked with Phyllis Schlafly and the Republican National Coalition for Life as a new, young Republican. We were promoting the pro-life cause.

The nominee was George H. W. Bush, and the party was generally united behind his candidacy. Defining the platform that year became a very contentious issue. The RINOs (Republicans in Name Only) that year wanted to remove the pro-life plank from the platform. It was a brutal battle, but ultimately the voice of the grass roots prevailed. We had to win in order to define what the GOP stood for and fought for. It was also a contract of sorts and a way for the grass roots to hold accountable the politicians they elected, as we did in 1996, when Bob Dole thumbed his nose at the hard-fought party platform. His campaign managers thought they could ignore the will of the people, and he was essentially cast out of GOP politics because of it. The message was clear: Respect the platform as the delegates voted it, or lose your base and lose your election.

In 2000 we continued our crusade, and not a single proabortion candidate entered the presidential race that year. The pro-life plank in the platform was adopted with little opposition.

The platform that year included language such as:

- "We say the unborn child has a fundamental individual right to life." (Section: "Upholding the Rights of All")

- "We support the traditional definition of 'marriage' as the legal union of one man and one woman." (Section: "Family Matters")
- "We defend the constitutional right to keep and bear arms." (Section: "Upholding the Rights of All")
- "We support the recognition of English as the nation's common language." (Section: "From Many, One")
- "We affirm the right of public schools, courthouses, and other public buildings to post copies of the Ten Commandments." (Section: "Justice and Safety")
- "American troops must never serve under United Nations command. Nor will they be subject to the jurisdiction of an International Criminal Court." (Section: "The United Nations")[5]

Since then we have added statements debunking environmentalism, suppressing illegal immigration, defending homeschooling, and calling for a ban on partial birth abortion. We even endorsed the Born Alive Infant Protection Act.

So what happened in 2008? Karl Rove and Reince Priebus discouraged candidate Mitt Romney from championing the party platform. Reince Priebus said in an interview with MSNBC during the Tampa convention, "This is the platform of the Republican Party. It is not the platform of Mitt Romney."[6] That is why Mitt Romney went the same way as Bob Dole. That is what happens to candidates who ignore the base of their party.

All is fair in love, war, and politics, and I believe it is every citizen's right to fight for whatever planks he or she wants to be included, or ignored, in the next party platform. The key is that a battle takes place; then we elect candidates who commit (and are held accountable) to honor the platform once elected. Some want the party to adopt or disregard certain messages. That is fine, but first they have to engage in the process and fight for their stance in the official platform. Regardless of your political views, the only power that adherents have over their elected officials once they are elected is their party platform. For this reason, grassroots activists must do three things:

1. Engage in the party process and fight for the planks they want in their party platform.
2. Hold their elected officials accountable.
3. Insist that their candidate campaign in accordance with the platform.

Ronald Reagan, the consummate conservative politician and hero of Republicans everywhere, said it best in his farewell speech from the Oval Office:

> God's hand is on America in a very preferential way. We have inherited a wonderful land of liberty and prosperity. It's our duty to safeguard our magnificent heritage. One way we do this is by adopting a Republican Party platform that designs the plan to rebuild the conservative movement, sets the standard for public officials, and then tries to hold them to it. We must use the procedures in the U.S. Constitution, and the mechanisms of self-government and of party politics to preserve our heritage.[7]

WHAT REAL WOMEN WANT

Famous shoe designer Christian Louboutin once said, "I wouldn't take it as a compliment if someone looked at one of my shoes and said, 'Oh, that looks like a comfortable shoe.' . . . There is a heel that is too high to walk in, certainly. But who cares? You don't have to walk in high heels."[8] I like heels because they are bold, even when uncomfortable. Real women want to be both beautiful and bold. We want to be at our best, but honest and authentic. We want to look our best while taking down our political opponents, not for materialistic reasons, but out of respect for ourselves. We don't want to talk about superficial things, like who we saw sitting with whom at the lunch table. There have been numerous studies about the confidence of a woman dressed for her goals. Sometimes that is decked in cammo with an AR-15 in her hands; sometimes that is torn jeans, a T-shirt, and a baby bottle in one hand with a child on her hip; and sometimes that is a dress and the perfect heels.

One recent Sunday morning, I flipped on the TV and the "alphabet soup" news emerged like cockroaches in the darkness. It was a day that ends in *y*, I suppose, so the networks were bashing conservative darling of the day, Ted Cruz.

That is nothing new. But I couldn't believe the context.

I choked on my coffee as I listened to two grown men (Bob Schieffer and Bob Woodward) gossiping like junior high girls about how Ted Cruz sat alone in the congressional lunchroom because he didn't go along with the leaders. Because he wouldn't do what the "in crowd" wanted him to do, they ostracized him like kids in a school cafeteria. He is the quintessential rebel.

Since when is "who sits with whom in the lunchroom" journalism? How does that pass the smell test for serious news analysis?

At that moment, if you'd looked across all of the potential candidates lining up for the next presidential election, Ted Cruz was the only one who was yet to take a position that was opposed to most Americans.

Most Americans loved him.

From his rugged, "real guy" look to his sincere, welcoming smile, to his candid tone and conservative message, Ted Cruz resonated with Americans. That is precisely why the news media wanted to drag him down. It is the MO of the media elite to attack the most viable candidates in the Republican Party. But it isn't about party politics as much as they would like for you to believe it is. It is about ideology. They know that at the core America is a right-of-center country. So they follow the same script every time. They attack the most attractive, "rightwardmost, viable candidate," as William F. Buckley put it.[9] They whittle away at the conservative darlings first. They attack the ones who really capture the hearts of Americans (e.g., Sarah Palin, Ron Paul, and Rick Santorum).

Their goal: rid the pool of presidential possibilities the American people like the most, especially those who are willing to speak up against the elite. Then, with the predictability of termites, in the final scene they attack the remaining platitudinous few (e.g., Romney, Dole, McCain, Bush) with the same parasitic vitriol. They ensure the victory goes to the elite of the elite—the one that can best be controlled.

Awakened Americans have seen this play, and they have the termite-chewed T-shirt to prove it.

My background is in psychology, and I can tell you that the old, white guys on *Face the Nation* might know what elite, old, white guys in the Beltway want, but they are totally out of touch with the pulse of the American woman. In their day, they may have been able to wink at the little filly and tell her what's good for her, but that doesn't work today. In their day, they might have been able to placate women with a "here's what's good for ya, honnneeey," but that will not work on real, twenty-first-century women.

Today's woman is living in the slag that the Washington elitists, like those on *Face the Nation* (and their bosses, the radical feminists), left behind. Thanks to their lack of any real masculinity, women today have little choice about working or not. The emasculation of Washington has also left women with few options to defend themselves against violent attack. What's more, many women are raising an entire generation of children alone—all thanks to the lack of real men on the American political scene.

Today, women looking for news instead get to hear about who sits alone in the Capitol lunchroom, and we get to know who some potential NFL recruit might sleep with next. The old, white guys in the elite media still flash back to their glory days and their "achievements" in skanky hotel rooms, but to most people, sex is not an achievement, and therefore, being gay is not an accomplishment.[10]

WHAT WOMEN *REALLY* WANT

If you ask conservative women today what they want, they'll tell you they want men. Real men.

WOMEN WANT MEN WHO ADVANCE THEIR ECONOMIC PROS-PERITY. This isn't out of greed; it is out of personal responsibility and true independence! They don't want to be told that if they aren't willing to fork over $1.5 million a day to Planned Parenthood, they will somehow lose their rights to their own bodies. Real women also know better than to think that the Fluked-up, fifteen-dollar freebie in birth control is worth relinquishing all other control over their lives, and that of their families. We have been reduced to walking uteruses, as a guest (Jordan Bosstick) on my show put it. Real women aren't dumb enough to buy that lie!

WOMEN WANT MEN WHO AREN'T AFRAID TO STAND ALONE. They want men who are willing to stand up to the status quo in Washington, DC, even if it means sitting alone in the lunchroom.

WOMEN WANT MEN WHO AREN'T AFRAID TO LET THEM THINK FOR THEMSELVES. Women want the freedom to make choices and even to fail, if that is what happens when they take a risk. They want government out of their bedrooms, their exam rooms, and their boardrooms! They want to be able to conduct their lives as they see fit, and to reach their full potential by trial and error. They want to be activists in their local communities without fear of retribution from the IRS, the NSA, the SEC, or invasions by the

TSA or the DOJ or the DOE. Government is just too powerful, and real women understand that the government large enough to give them everything they (supposedly) want, is also big enough to take away everything they have (Jefferson).

WOMEN WANT MEN WHO WILL DO THEIR OWN JOBS. Even if that means taking a hard, lonely line against the peer pressure of those with the power to destroy them, women want men who will get the job done. Women I talk to today often say that their first love, like mine, is being a wife and mother. That is by God's own design. But today, so many women must forgo that dream to enter the workplace (because flawed government policy has failed to make a one-income family a reality anymore), the political arena (because not enough good men are willing to make the sacrifice to run), and even the battlefield (where the implications of the failed military experiment are just coming to light).

WOMEN WANT MEN WHO WILL LISTEN. They want men who will take their values of life, liberty, and the pursuit of happiness all the way to the Oval Office. Women want men who care about more than football (#RollTide!), and who will spend their time and resources on causes that make a difference.

WHAT WOMEN REALLY *DON'T* WANT

WOMEN DON'T WANT TO BE ENSLAVED. Not by welfare, or dependence, or a subtle threat that if they don't advocate baby killing, they might lose some right to have sex when they want to. Women don't want to be bribed by fifteen-dollar-a-month birth control. We know we are worth far more, and we won't be bought like slaves in an Islamic country.

WOMEN DON'T WANT TO BE PLACATED OR PATRONIZED. We are tired of the old lines from a government that said they would "take care of" us, and only leaves us standing alone with no care at all—nothing but a number.

WOMEN DON'T WANT TO BE LABELED. We don't want to be parsed by old or young, rich or poor, black or white, fat or thin, and we don't want to be pitted against men. Real women like men. We are more than our gender, and we expect our men to appreciate what is real and feminine about us. Politics shouldn't be about division. Real politics is about standing together for the values we share as Americans, and finding common ground through adult dialogue, civil discourse.

WOMEN DON'T WANT TO BE INVADED. Women don't want Uncle Sam in their exam rooms. They have seen what government—the NSA, TSA, IRS, SEC—does with their private information, and they want no part of Obamacare.

Sadly, some of the women who don't mind being enslaved, patronized, or invaded have altogether given up on men, thanks to men like the old, white guys on *Face the Nation* who have been running things for so long. Maybe those guys don't want to sit with Ted in the lunchroom, and they would rather sit at the "cool kids table," smiling about gay football players. But I'm pretty sure Ted could find company in the cafeteria with the cool chicks who know what women really want. And he would probably rather sit with them than with Schieffer or Woodward, anyway. Wouldn't you?

How can real women get involved? How can they make a difference? They can run for office, volunteer to help with a campaign, write op-ed pieces, start a blog, talk to their friends and family, call their senators, and best of all, vote. Both the left and the right try to rally the troops to get out and vote. That is what drives the country.

If the shoe fits, baby, buy it in every color! But if you fit in the crowd, RUN! Consider this: during the 2000 campaign *Rolling Stone* sent out David Foster to find out why so many Americans liked Senator John McCain. Maybe Foster was worried that McCain might have a chance because what he wrote to his audience about getting out there to vote was inspired:

If you are bored and disgusted by politics and don't bother to vote, you are in effect voting for the entrenched Establishments of the two major parties who, rest assured are not dumb, and who are keenly aware that it is in their interests to keep you disgusted and bored and cynical and to give you every possible reason to stay at home doing one-hitters and watching *MTV Spring Break* on Primary Day. By all means stay home if you want, but don't bullsh** yourself that you're not voting. In reality, there is *no such thing as not voting*: you either vote by voting, or you vote by staying home and tacitly doubling the value of some Diehard's vote.[11]

Only 50 percent of churchgoing people even vote in a general election. For churchgoing women, those numbers are even more dismal—around 20 percent, according to Pew Research.

I don't want to dish on my girlfriends, but when I have the "why aren't you involved in the politics that determine how you leave this world to your children?" conversation, their answer is almost always the same. They don't want to make enemies. Politics is ugly, unseemly. Women don't like war, and politics feels like war. I submit that it is indeed a war. And I further challenge those not politically involved that voting is *not enough*—that is, if you care about your own future, plan to partake of freedom, and care if your children and grandchildren get to enjoy the same freedoms you have today.

I found this quote by John Stuart Mill yesterday in a barber shop on Coronado Island: "War is an ugly thing, but not the ugliest of things; the decayed and degraded state of moral and patriotic feeling which thinks nothing is worth a war, is worse. A man who has nothing which he cares more about than he does about his personal safety is a miserable creature who has no chance at being free, unless made and kept so by the exertions of better men than himself."

So I am apparently not the only conservative left in deep Southern California. And I know where to send my husband for a haircut now.

It is hard to be vulnerable to losing friends by taking a stand, but I will submit to you that you will be better for it. And I am certain your children will be better for your having taken a stand.

One of my favorite reads for apolitical comic relief is Dr. Isaiah Hankel's blog, *Experiments in Cheeky Science*. Hankel, who has a PhD in anatomy and cell biology, shares valuable tips as well as his own stories of how being a waiter made him successful in business, and how wrestling in high school helped him grapple with life. In his post "15 Benefits of Being an Intelligent Misfit," Hankel contends that fitting in is actually a catastrophe.

According to Hankel, who is a Fortune 500 consultant and a celebrated expert in the biotechnology industry, successful people avoid "swarm think" because "swarms don't think; they react." Studies on groupthink, or herd mentality, show that humans and animals both respond to environmental changes with exceptionally low levels of cognition. Therefore, "large groups," he says, "are often led, not by the proactive choices of each individual, but by a large collection of dull responses." Thus, fitting in puts you in the middle of a big, dull blob that can really only react.

Hankel goes on to say that groups of friends usually like you only if you are doing what they are doing, and if you deviate from the group, you will face rejection. That, by definition, is not friendship.

Further studies indicate that even adding intelligent people to your group won't help you be more successful. "A group of 200 people," says Hankel, "will not perform any better whether 10 or 100 of them are intelligent." The benefits lie in being different, in "sticking out," even. Sticking out will ultimately result in better friendships, higher pay scales, increased creativity, and even more time.[12] The lesson here is obvious: Aside from the intrinsic reward for having the courage to take a stand, there are real, practical rewards too!

As Andy Hunt said in his book *Pragmatic Thinking and Learning,* "Only dead fish go with the flow."[13]

Real women don't go with the flow.

One of the ways women can swim against the current is through unrelenting compassion and empathy. There is one thing real women do best, and that is love. We know what is best for others, yet our real power lies not in telling them, but in demonstrating it. As Margaret Thatcher said, "Power is like being a lady. If you have to tell people you are, you aren't." Just because we know what works in the world, the answer isn't shouting that in the face of everyone we see, but in loving them and waiting for them to ask what it is about us that is different. And finally, just because someone doesn't believe what we believe, that is no excuse not to love them anyway.

I love Mother Teresa's perspective on this. This is her "Anyway" poem, written on the wall of her home for children in Calcutta:

People are often unreasonable, illogical and self centered; forgive them anyway.

If you are kind, people may accuse you of selfish, ulterior motives; be kind anyway.

If you are successful, you will win some false friends and some true enemies; succeed anyway.

If you are honest and frank, people may cheat you; be honest and frank anyway.

What you spend years building, someone could destroy overnight; build anyway.

If you find serenity and happiness, they may be jealous; be happy anyway.

The good you do today, people will often forget tomorrow; do good anyway.

Give the world the best you have, and it may never be enough; give the world the best you've got anyway.

In the final analysis, it is between you and God; it was never between you and them anyway.

I would add that doormats do only one thing well, and that is getting walked on. Don't be a doormat. Sometimes love is tough too. Sometimes it means teaching a bully a lesson by hitting back. Sometimes love means telling a friend the difficult truth. Sometimes it means standing up all alone, raising your hand knowing someone will slap it down, or speaking the truth, even when your voice shakes (think Maggie Kuhn). Sometimes love is war. Prepare for battle.

9

TO WIN BACK HOLLYWOOD

by MORGAN BRITTANY

Can we save our country and bring some sense back to our culture? Sometimes I shake my head and ask, are Hollywood and the entertainment industry a lost cause? I ponder my fifty-plus-year journey, where I witnessed the good, the bad, and the ugly in this town. I know that Hollywood, the music industry, and all of its ancillary divisions are capable of creating amazing products. We have all seen it; the ability is there. There are brilliant ideas out there, and incredible talent, and I am always excited when I see it.

The actors and directors are just as brilliant as they have always been, and I am constantly amazed at how new talent emerges and rises to the top. There is more opportunity now than ever before, with all of the avenues available to view entertainment. That can be a blessing as well as a curse. Anything and everything can be found on cable, the Internet, your smartphone, video games, etc. It is extremely difficult to monitor what is out there, and the world of entertainment can be a minefield for you and your children.

I must admit, I love to sit down in a darkened movie theater with popcorn in hand and escape into another world for a couple of uninterrupted hours. Film can take you anywhere; it propels you into other worlds. It takes you to the past or the future, makes you laugh and cry, and touches you in ways you never thought possible. Music can do the same. How many times have you turned on the radio and heard a song that immediately triggers a memory? The entertainment industry has provided us with an abundance of sensual pleasures, and they have the ability to expand on that with more technological advances every day.

I hear from a lot of people that they wish they could go back to the good old days of film and TV. Well, I am afraid we will never return to the "good old days." That was then; this is now. The reality is that our world is not what it was, nor, frankly, should it be. Progress is inevitable, and we all welcome it in one way or another. My main concern is not that we are rapidly advancing and progressing with new ideas; I welcome that. I am more concerned about what ideas we are advancing and progressing toward.

As far back as Plato, we have been warned that people are manipulable and irrational when they fall under the thrall of a talented bard, and whose voice is more persuasive than the entertainment industry's? It creates "legends" and "stars" that are more illusion than reality, yet adoring fans desperately seek to imitate them. Why do you think that young girls dress and act like their favorite singing or movie star? They believe that doing so will make people look at and admire them. But they have created an illusion. This has been going on for decades and is nothing new. As Thomas Paine said in *Common Sense,* "A long habit of not thinking a thing wrong, gives it a superficial appearance of being right, and raises at first a formidable outcry in defence of custom. But the tumult soon subsides. Time makes more converts than reason."

At the turn of the last century, the Gibson Girl, drawn by Charles Dana Gibson, illustrated the ideal woman. In the '20s it was Clara Bow. The 1950s gave us Elizabeth Taylor and Marilyn Monroe. People always emulate icons and will continue to do so. On the darker side, how many times have we seen a mass killer who emulates a film or video game character?

Young people idolize stars, models, musicians, and sports figures. They look at their actions and follow their example. Unfortunately today, most public figures are setting bad examples, and the media is exploiting and rewarding them. I don't think there has ever been a time in this country's history that has rewarded and glorified the dysfunctional more than now. So, the question is, how do we manage this issue and turn our culture around?

First, consider the goal of mass media and the entertainment industry. We all know that the bottom line is to make money. Anything that can be done to capture the attention of a viewer or listener will ensure a larger gain for the producer. In the 1940s and '50s it was the extravagant musicals that came out of MGM. After that it was the epic stories, like *Cleopatra* and *How the West Was Won*, in CinemaScope and Cinerama. The industry brought out everything it had to lure people into the theaters. Once people grew tired of that novelty, something new needed to be offered. Over the years, because of many left-leaning influences, vulgarity, violence, coarse language, and graphic sexual images that were previously hidden became mainstream and were offered to capture people's attention. The coarsening of our society had begun.

If you look back at history, barbaric acts, brutal competitions, and spectacles were performed in front of crowds of cheering spectators.

Fights to the death were commonplace in ancient Rome, and the "thumbs up, thumbs down" verdict elicited yeas or nays from the crowd. If you think about it though, eons later, whether it is high culture or popular culture, the goal is to keep people engaged with what they are seeing or hearing and have them return for more.

There is no question that America's entertainment industry has always been the powerhouse in the world. Its pure economic power is undeniable. Billions of dollars in entertainment product is exported every year to every country in the world. Even in Iran, it is possible to gain access to books by Danielle Steele and John Grisham.

Our world is not as it was in the 1940s or even as it was in the naughts. America no longer lives in a vacuum, creating images, music, and stories that reflect *just* our values and culture. We now live in a global world, interconnected with every other person and country on this planet. Because of this, we can no longer have blinders on and see life only through *our* eyes. This is the world we live in, and now have to navigate.

Every country around the world has its own regional entertainment and culture. Every day however, those regional cultures are being overtaken because of the availability of entertainment from around the world. Before the advent of the computer, smartphones, and other technological miracles, it took longer for countries to be influenced by others. I remember vividly, after the fall of the Soviet Union, receiving fan mail for *Dallas* from East Germany and the Soviet-bloc countries. They conveyed the fact that even though fans were told by the state that this was an unrealistic view of the world, that no one lived with such luxury and wealth, they wanted to know more. They were ravenous for information about other societies and cultures.

There is no doubt that entertainment has become a much more powerful industry. It drives the global economy and influences cultures across the globe. Now American influence is everywhere. It has permeated most of the countries around the world through our exporting of film, television, music, books, games, fashion, and so forth. Other countries are competing, however, with their own product. Countries like China, India, and South Korea have a booming and profitable entertainment industry. Where years ago, the product coming to the United States from these countries was subpar, now we are seeing first-class acting and production value. Take for example *Crouching Tiger, Hidden Dragon*. This film received high accolades and many awards. The brilliance of these countries is that they recruit talent from the United States, work with them, learn from them, and then utilize that knowledge for themselves. In that way, they can make sure that their cultures survive because they aren't just getting American product and values. They can produce products keeping their own values and morals intact.

At first, the exporting of American entertainment was seen to be an awakening for the rest of the world to transition from tradition to modernity. It was a window into how economically underdeveloped countries could prosper. In theory this seemed to be a good idea, but this theory was based on a model of the Western World that devalued their traditions. I often wonder if the filmmakers and producers really think about the message they are sending to the world with their products. My experience is that perhaps they *used* to, but as the market exploded over the past few decades, they gave little thought to how we, America, look to the world.

If perhaps America exported products that extolled the virtues of freedom, independence, individuality, and self-sufficiency, we would give a positive and uplifting image to the world. That used to be the norm in film, and was the reason that millions of people dreamed of coming to America. You need not hit people over the head with propaganda, but it is a way to empower people and open them up to finding their own identities. One can only hope that somehow Middle Eastern women will see that there are other options available for them through the voice of freedom.

I have recently found that some of the popular programming coming from the British is full of conservative values. They seem to have found a way to intrigue us with their television exports. The enormous success of *Downton Abbey* and *Sherlock* is evidence of that. Another series, *Mr. Selfridge* is gaining popularity as well. It is interesting to note that these shows, especially *Downton* and *Selfridge*, have incredibly talented casts, and the production values are superb. Most interesting, however, are the story lines and the messages that are relayed through the plots. Both manage to intertwine good and evil characters, human frailties, and sacrifice. It is refreshing to watch characters give of themselves for another, stand up for right, show tremendous loyalty, and when confronted with a pregnancy, not choose abortion. Characters in these series show remorse for wrongdoing, pay the price for dishonesty, and have a love of home and country. Of course, the time period for these pieces is the late 1800s into the 1920s, and life was different then, but even so, the producers and writers could easily have chosen to celebrate the negative, but did not.

This is what needs to change in Hollywood and the entertainment industry as a whole. It *can* be done, and not in an old-fashioned way. We have an incredibly talented pool of writers, directors, and actors who believe in conservative values. They create wonderful scripts that tell heartwarming, heroic stories, and do it in a modern, cutting-edge way. The message *can* entertain, and at the same time utilize the best talent that Hollywood has to offer.

I recently saw a film called *Ride Along*. Being in the "older" demographic, I wasn't particularly interested in seeing a "younger buddy cop movie," but my husband had worked on it and told me that I might be surprised. Indeed I was. The film centered on an older cop whose sister is going to marry a rather unfocused young guy who is trying to get into the police force. It is a typical comedy, very much geared to the young male, but as I watched it, I was surprised by the dialogue. The characters had good values and stood up and did the right thing. Instead of turning into corrupt criminals, these guys were heroes. Yes, there was the typical car chase, along with "shoot 'em up" scenes and street dialogue, but even these were done in a tactful way that appealed to the audience. The actors were engaging as well, really connecting with the young audience. It was a brilliant move on the part of the director and writer because the film, with a budget of $25 million, has now made nearly $130 million. Wrapped in the package of a modern-day action film, *Ride Along* also managed to squeeze in some subliminal messages. Hopefully they will get through.

There is a tremendous opportunity for the entertainment industry to champion good and honorable values, but instead they tend to export values that many Americans don't embrace. Reality shows that portray Americans as stupid and materialistic are being seen by many countries. Instead of creating product that glorifies heroes, hard work, love, and compassion, we send television shows featuring people who are "famous for being famous" and hype their greedy, narcissistic lifestyles. This is tearing down the image that America has built and trashing it to the rest of the world.

I recently spoke to a twenty-one-year-old girl from Indonesia. She met and married an American Marine and moved to California. She had grown up watching American films and television. Her idea of what the United States was like had been molded from the programming she had seen. She told me that her brother, who was a bit rebellious, loved American music and was becoming a fan of rap "music." When I asked her what her initial thoughts about

America were before she came here, she told me she had feared the country was violent and tumultuous. She never thought she would fit in because American women were not like her; they were only concerned with appearance, clothes, money, and sex. Worse, she felt that no one was honest or trustworthy in America, and that money, sex, and drugs made you popular.

Many women in Indonesia were not treated the best when she was young, she told me. There were still not many opportunities for a woman to be independent and free. But growing up, she heard her mother tell stories of how women in America were honored and cherished and given opportunities to achieve whatever they imagined. That was in complete contrast to what she was seeing herself in many American films and television shows. Most American men she had seen in films were preoccupied with sex, and their treatment of women was disrespectful, so when she met her future husband, she was hesitant. He proved to her that her fears were unfounded, and soon they moved to the United States. She told me that her attitudes toward America changed when she realized that the majority of people were *not* like what she had been led to believe. She saw good values, honesty, and faith in the people in the community where they settled, and she was amazed to find out how right her mother had been.

Today, Hollywood and the music industry know that the majority of their money is made globally. To continue to grab the biggest piece of the international market, they need to produce product that translates and resonates with everyone. Car crashes and chases, huge special effects, and superhero and fantasy films generate enormous box-office revenues because they are generic and can be understood without dialogue or translation. It is not necessarily important that music have meaningful lyrics anymore as long as it has the *heartbeat rhythm.* The melody and structure is unimportant as long as the incessant pounding beat is there. From Abu Dhabi to Tokyo to Singapore and Ukraine, the same music is popular in the nightclubs.

It has taken about one hundred years for the culture to be changed into what it is today. The leftist agenda has been at work trying to mold it into their "ideal" in a methodical, patient way. It certainly is not an easy task to change it back. But I think it *can* be done. It has to start with all of us.

There is already a cultural shift going on in America. The progressives don't want you to think so, and the media tries to downplay it, but they know that the unrest being felt and now spoken about is bubbling up. A majority of people are *still* practicing some sort of religious belief, even though the atheists want you to believe that is untrue. A majority of the people still know right from wrong, and they believe in honor and integrity. Even abortion, the holy grail for progressives, is becoming less and less popular among Americans in general and women specifically.

The pendulum always swings, and when one side steps over the line, there is always pushback. It is not as though this hasn't happened before; things were wild and crazy in the Roaring Twenties. The key to changing our culture is within our reach, but we have to be smart.

Remember how long it took us to get here? Over decades people were conditioned to believe and accept things that went against their nature. The unacceptable became acceptable. The media were the driving force in perpetuating new and shocking ideas, but they hammered away and made it mainstream and normal. They are brilliant at conditioning the masses. They made their ideas attractive, especially to the young, who are always open to new and exciting notions. Not all changes have been negative, though. The media were right in pushing to end racism and sexism. Those were extremely positive changes that needed to be fought for and won.

We need to use these same tactics in reversing some of the negative effects that have become embedded in our society. When we see an injustice or a stifling of our basic liberties, we need to raise our voices and be heard. I am not saying that we stand up and condemn everything that offends us. That definitely will *not* work. But we should start a dialogue and open up the conversation. Starting within our own families and with our own children, we need to understand what page everyone is on and open up the floor. Discuss issues of right and wrong. Find out why your children think the way they do about issues, but don't condemn or preach. Having an open discussion without judgment can open the door to advance your cause.

We need to support the people within the media who are speaking up for conservative values: truth, liberty, and freedom from oppressive regulations and taxes. Rally around them, buy their products, and patronize their sponsors. Watch television, see films, buy books, and purchase products from people who are willing to support your values and the values of America. We have seen this sort of support in action, most specifically with Chick-fil-A. Thousands of people felt that this company was being persecuted for the beliefs of its founder, and they voiced their opposition. It had nothing to do with what the media spouted. The people defending Chick-fil-A had nothing against gays or gay rights; they just stood up for the right of the company's founder to have his private beliefs, which hurt no one.

We have an uphill battle against the mainstream media. Every chance they get they will demonize us and turn us into something we are not. They will slap the uncaring, greedy, racist, homophobe label on us, but we need to counter it. Don't let them get away with it. *They are the bully on the playground,* not us. They are the ones who want to stifle our voices and take away our power. We are not haters, we are not intolerant, and we won't be labeled. We cannot allow that to happen.

Hollywood has been one of the biggest reasons political correctness has a stranglehold on this country. In everything they do, with every celebrity interview, they will try to push their idea of utopia and *fairness* on us. As long as you agree with them and follow their lead, you won't encounter any problems. But heaven forbid a conservative actress speaks out for a Republican candidate. She is vilified on every social media site in the world. Speak out against global warming, and you are ridiculed as an ignorant fool. Believe in traditional marriage, and you are a hater. Oppose abortion, and you automatically hate women, even if you are one! There are elements in Hollywood that have no tolerance for conservative Americans. They feel that America is not special or outstanding.

When we begin to turn the cultural ship around, they will scream and yell all the louder. Their voices are becoming more shrill even now because more and more of us are seeing the truth and pushing back. They will try everything to silence us including lobbying for legislation or encouraging executive orders if they can.

It's been a long time coming, but we are shining the light on Hollywood and the media. In the glare of truth, they will cower and realize that, yes, we are a force to be reckoned with.

DILIGENCE AND TENACITY: STAYING THE COURSE

by ANN-MARIE MURRELL

A conservative is someone who stands athwart history, yelling Stop, at a time when no one is inclined to do so, or to have much patience with those who so urge it.[1] —WILLIAM F. BUCKLEY JR.

Whoever created the "silent majority" moniker for Republicans either had it in for the GOP or didn't realize the trouble it would cause. As a matter of fact, I'll go so far as to say that being so blooming silent is one of the main reasons we're in the mess we're in today.

It's understandable why the left is afraid of us now. For decades, they had been able to rule the roost mostly unchallenged in almost every aspect of life: government, academia, and the media. They relished our silence and took full advantage of the fact that they completely owned the narrative. By not speaking up and standing up for ourselves, we were allowing only one side of the debate to ever be heard by most of the free world.

And still, Republicans maintained—and almost seemed to take

pride in—the title "silent majority" while the ACLU and progressives gained a stronghold in America. They removed crosses from hillsides and the Ten Commandments from office buildings. Prayer was taken out of schools, as was God from most public places. Other than Rush Limbaugh and a handful of talk radio hosts who came around in the 1980s, and Fox News in 1996, no "regular" Americans were speaking up—until the Tea Party came along and changed the world.

Strangely, as much as the left is terrified of the Republican Party, the Republican Party seems equally terrified of the Tea Party, and the fact that the Tea Party movement is still mostly made up of Republicans makes for a very strange and complex dichotomy. So one of the main questions I'm asked when I speak at events across the country is, how can we pull our party together to win elections? It's a very good question.

TEENAGERS AND GRANDPARENTS

To many Republicans, the Tea Party movement represents wild, out-of-control teenagers who are wrapped up in the excitement of their youth and their passions. There really wasn't any *easing* into this activism/Tea Party thing; people went from being completely silent, seemingly passive and indifferent, to screaming, shouting, rallying, protesting, writing, blogging. And PolitiChick-ing. These were things that simply had never been done within the GOP.

Conversely, many Tea Partiers think of the GOP as geriatric grandparents, old and out of touch.

The good news is that as divided as we may seem, unless or until a third Tea Party emerges, we are still mostly registered Republicans. We're still fighting for the same cause—the United States of America—and we still believe that the Constitution is the foundation of our country. Some very simple ideas can help us begin the healing process between the Grand Old Party and the Tea Party activists and win almost all our elections. It's really not as difficult or insurmountable as it may seem.

THE PACHYDERMS

In any disagreement, one of the first things you can do to start healing is show consideration and understanding about what the other side is going through. Ask yourself, Why are they angry? Are they angry, or perhaps just frightened? Are they frightened of change? What type of change are they afraid of, and why?

In the case of the Republican Party, consider, if you will, John and Mary Pachyderm. Mr. and Mrs. Pachyderm have been retired for decades. They have lived full, rewarding lives. Their three children are grown and live in other states, with children of their own—altogether, nine teenagers, to be exact. The Pachyderms eat lunch every day at noon and dinner every evening at 5:00 sharp. They have a regimented routine of television programs, mostly consisting of Fox News and the Weather Channel. Their biggest outing of the week is to go to church on Sundays, and perhaps have lunch with friends afterward. They only see their children and grandchildren once a year around Christmas.

One day, without notice or advance warning, all nine teenage grandchildren show up at the Pachyderms' front door. The teens had grown concerned that their grandparent's lives were too boring and needed change. "We're here to help you!" yell the teenagers. "We're here to make things better!"

Mr. and Mrs. Pachyderm are initially happy to see their grandchildren, thrilled with their exuberance . . . until they realize the kids have no plans to leave.

Everything in the Pachyderms' lives is turned upside down. The teenagers eat whenever they're hungry, which seems to be

24/7. They change the television channel—even when *The Five* on Fox is coming on. The Pachyderms love their grandchildren, and vice versa—but they don't know how to cope with such massive changes. So after a month of having their lives turned upside down, the Pachyderms get angry. They lash out; they call their beloved grandchildren names like "hobbits" and "wackobirds."

The teenagers, being teenagers, don't understand why their grandparents are angry, but they, too, react in anger. In their minds, they came to take care of their grandparents, to make their lives fuller and richer, so they don't understand why their fervor isn't welcomed and appreciated.

Bottom line: the Pachyderms have already experienced the exuberance of youth; they are tired. They are ready to rest.

This doesn't mean you get rid of the grandchildren, *or* the grandparents—and *this* is where we are today, folks.

Like it or not, we are all still family. We are all still fighting the same battle.

In February 2014 I was in North Carolina and met with state representative Chris Malone. As he talked with me about the economic problems in his state, he compared the path to recovery to a ship's course: "Consider that North Carolina is a huge ocean liner," he said. "You can't turn the economy around on a dime, but it's a wide arc that gets you in the right direction." The other side wants to continue that path of stagnation and high debt, which we have either already rid ourselves of or are currently getting under control. We can do better. It's a great story.

"It's a wide arc that gets you in the right direction." That's a fitting metaphor for the road to America's cultural recovery. It took us decades to get to this place in history where our liberty is being replaced with tyranny—so it will take a wide arc to turn us around. We have already come light-years from where we were just a short while ago. It wasn't that long ago that we all believed ABC/CBS/NBC were legitimate, unbiased news sources. Until relatively recently, there were zero conservative websites, and only a handful of conservative talk radio shows were in existence—and we didn't even question the *New York Times* and *Newsweek*.

If we care about saving our party and ultimately winning elections, patience, organization, and clear-headed thinking is the compromise that needs to take place between the Tea Party and the GOP. Like the family that we are, we can—and should—be able to sit down together and hash out our differences, and find ways to work together instead of against each other. From everything I've personally seen from both the GOP and the Tea Party, this is mainly all about growing pains, like Pachyderm's teenage grandchildren.

Change is never easy, but to evolve and grow, it's vital. Yes, the Republican Party has grown stagnant. Politicians have gotten too cushy in DC, and they lost touch with who works for whom. The Tea Party movement, as brash and loud as it may seem, needed to happen. The people needed a voice, and eventually, once both sides calm down and learn to live and work together, I believe we will become a powerful force that can and *will* save America.

RESEARCH, REACH OUT, AND RUN!

Like many Americans, before I became obsessively involved in the world of politics, when it came to elections—big and small—I simply voted for whoever had an *R* in front of their names (or a *D* when I was a Democrat). I had determined that someone, somewhere, had figured out who the Rs should be, and who was I to question that authority?

Now I question it. I question everything and everyone and every issue, and so should you—and you should do so far in advance, not only on Election Day. In 2012 I studied, researched, and wrote about all of the GOP candidates. I watched every debate in both the primaries and general election and talked to conservatives in each of the candidate's states to find out what they thought of them. By the time Election Day came around and the contest was ultimately between Mitt Romney and Barack Obama, there was no choice. I was not about to give Obama my vote, which I would have done had I not voted for his opponent. Ultimately, conservatives (or Republicans) had simply not done enough to ensure that their candidate won the election. They also believe not enough had been done to ensure a true conservative Republican candidate was on the ballot in the first place.

So what can all of us do in the months or years leading up to elections? Research, reach out, and if you're the right person, run for office!

The days of being passive Republicans are over. It's not enough to simply cast a vote anymore (although that is critical, of course). Everyone is needed for a multitude of things and every gift and talent a person possesses is needed like never before.

The Democrats became deft at organizing when Saul Alinsky hit town. His simple, easy-to-follow list of rules became the guidelines that people like Hillary Clinton and Barack Obama have diligently followed. We don't need to become them, but we absolutely need to get organized and be alert to the tricks of the other side. And Lord help us! They do not play fair.

RESEARCH EVERYTHING

When it comes to local elections, I think of my vote as a sacred gift I am giving to a potential leader, so I treat it as such. In my state of California, I research every candidate, especially the ones whose election can potentially make a major impact on the life of all Californians. In the 2014 California governor's race, several people who stepped in (and out) of the race were much more like Democrats than the Republicans they claimed to be. So for me, the only man who stood for everything I believed could make that "wide arc" to save California was Assemblyman Tim Donnelly. Of course, it helped that my husband and I have personally known Tim and his family for years. I've interviewed him multiple times and have seen him in action in Sacramento. But I don't support Tim Donnelly because he's a friend; I support him because I know what's in his heart: a deep love and respect for California. Originally, Tim Donnelly, like George Washington, never wanted to be a politician, but injustice and government oppression compelled him to get involved. That's what it's all about.

REACH OUT!

Please, please, please, I implore you: even if you consider them "strong" conservatives, don't assume your family members and/or friends are voting. Odds are, they're not. If every registered Republican had voted for Romney in 2012, we would not be fighting this creeping totalitarianism we're dealing with now.

My theory that the Democratic Party created the phrase "Never talk religion and politics at the table" comes into play here. We've all got to talk more often—and without whispering—about religion and politics. Yes, at the dinner table. Yes, in line at Chick-fil-A, or the car wash, or any other public place you may be. The days of hiding ourselves are over. Be loud; be proud; be conservative!

Of course, when it comes to voting, people think, *I'm just one person; my vote won't count anyway*. But consider the snowflake. Individually, they are delicate, powerless, and they disappear with the slightest touch; however, together snowflakes can create an impassible, unstoppable avalanche. Of course our individualism is important; it's who we are as Republicans. But if we continue the isolationism routine, digging our heels so far in the sand that we bury ourselves, we're going to disappear like a snowflake on a windshield—which is what the Democratic Party is absolutely counting on.

Right away, start working on any election that is coming your way. Sharron Angle, who ran against Harry Reid in 2010, learned from her mistakes and is now actively working on nationwide voting tactics. In Sharron's election, Harry Reid was criticized for using busses to bring voters (okay, Union voters) to the polls. But Angle suggests every state should do the same—and why not? Offering easy, worry-free ways to get to your local polling place is a very simple solution for people who don't have transportation, live in nursing homes or perhaps use rideshare for their work and can't get away.

Also the moment that election is over, start working on the next one. Our party has been notorious for putting elections away like Christmas decorations, forgetting about them until the next year. The other side never stops working on elections. Never. So get your friends and family involved, because you are needed like never before.

RUN FOR OFFICE!

As far as I'm concerned, someone having "years of political experience" isn't a good thing anymore and won't necessarily earn you my vote. My personal criteria for someone who can and should run for office are the following:

A CANDIDATE MUST BE EXTREMELY INTELLIGENT. You've got to be quick on your feet and able to answer any question at any time on just about any subject. Sometimes it takes an extremely intelligent person to say, "I don't know."

A CANDIDATE MUST BE INFORMED. You need to know *all* the issues, including foreign and world politics, even if you're running for a state or local office.

A CANDIDATE MUST HAVE A PASSIONATE LOVE FOR AMERICA. This should go without saying, but after the Obama administration, it must be repeated.

A CANDIDATE CAN HAVE NO SKELETONS! I'm personally sick to death of all the creepy skeletons that seem to constantly pop out of politicians' closets. If you have any, please, oh, please, do not ever run for office (unless you run as a Democrat).

That's it. Easy. Now, let's get out there and save the world.

WE'VE ALREADY COME A LONG WAY, BABY!

It wasn't that long ago that the name Walter Cronkite meant "journalism" and "truth." His closing statement, "And that's the way it is," sort of put a period at the end of the nightly news. If Cronkite said it, there was no need to question or talk back, because that *was* the way it *was*. Even now, I still sometimes hear people talk about the "good old days," when journalism was filled with "decent, honest" reporters and when you could trust whatever your TV news broadcasters told you.

Like most others, I, too, believed anything and everything Walter Cronkite and all the other news leaders of the day had to say. If it came out of the mouths of Tom Brokaw or Dan Rather, it had to be true, right? Well, no. I also used to think I would grow up to marry Bobby Sherman, and that didn't happen either. In both the nightly news and in my *Tiger Beat*–induced love life, that fantasy-crusher reality finally took hold and made me see that none of the "journalists" of my childhood necessarily had the same principles or character as my family and me.

What I now realize is that having "father figure" Cronkite say, "And that's the way it is," in his velvety yet commanding voice, was a brilliant way to mass hypnotize America. So who were the men writing the nightly news back then? In his later years, Walter Cronkite finally came out of his statist closet and admitted some rather stunning revelations about his so-called journalistic integrity. The Media Research Center chronicles comments Cronkite made throughout the years about everything from abortion and his hippie-esque antiwar stance to the flat-out admission that "all journalists are liberal." Here are a few Cronkite-isms from over the years:[2]

ON LIBERALISM: "I know liberalism isn't dead in this country. It simply has, temporarily we hope, lost its voice. . . . We know that unilateral action in Grenada and Tripoli was wrong. We know that 'Star Wars' means uncontrollable escalation of the arms race. We know that the real threat to democracy is the half of the nation in poverty. We know that no one should tell a woman she has to bear an unwanted child. . . . Gawd Almighty, we've got to shout these truths in which we believe from the housetops. Like that scene in the movie 'Network,' we've got to throw open our windows and shout these truths to the streets and the heavens. And I bet we'll find more windows are thrown open to join the chorus than we'd ever dreamed possible."

ON THE NEW WORLD ORDER: "If we are to avoid that catastrophe [a nuclear World War III], a system of world order—preferably a system of world government—is mandatory. The proud nations someday will see the light and, for the common good and their own survival, yield up their precious sovereignty, just as America's thirteen colonies did two centuries ago. When we finally come to our senses and establish a world executive and parliament of nations, thanks to the Nuremburg precedent we will already have in place the fundamentals for the third branch of government, the judiciary."

ON THE NEED FOR THE UNITED STATES TO "GIVE UP SOME OF OUR SOVEREIGNTY" TO THE UN: "It seems to many of us that if we are to avoid the eventual catastrophic world conflict we must strengthen the United Nations as a first step toward a world government patterned after our own government with a legislature, executive and judiciary, and police to enforce its international laws and keep the peace. To do that, of course, we Americans will have to give up some of our sovereignty. . . .

"Time will not wait. Democracy, civilization itself, is at stake. Within the next few years we must change the basic structure of our global community from the present anarchic system of war and ever more destructive weaponry to a new system governed by a democratic U.N. federation. . . .

"Our failure to live up to our obligations to the U.N. is led by a handful of willful senators who choose to pursue their narrow, selfish political objectives at the cost of our nation's conscience. They pander to and are supported by the Christian Coalition and the rest of the religious right wing."

9/11 WAS *WHOSE* FAULT? "I think very definitely that foreign policy could have caused what has happened [September 11, 2001 terrorist attacks]. . . . It certainly should be apparent now—it should be, for goodness sakes, understood now, but it is not—that the problem is this great division between the rich and the poor in the world. We represent the rich. . . . Most of these other nations of Africa, Asia and South America and Central America are very, very poor. . . . This is a revolution in effect around the world. A revolution is in place today. We are suffering from a revolution of the poor and have-nots against the rich and haves and that's us."

And finally, be sure to check out the YouTube video of Mr. Cronkite receiving the Norman Cousins Global Governance Award in 2006. Especially note around 1:26, when Cronkite ridicules Christianity and then says, "Well, join me—I'm glad to sit here at the right hand of Satan." At the end, then First Lady Hillary Clinton also makes a statement commending Cronkite's "leadership."[3]

So when you get discouraged and think we're not moving fast enough, not making enough progress, keep in mind we are still brand-new at this fight. The other guys have been battling us for decades, and in many cases, like Cronkite, they were fighting us even when we didn't know we were fighting. Now we know. And *that's* the way it is.

WHY I BELIEVE WE WILL WIN

Back in my struggling actress–single mom days, I sometimes had to pay for gas with a handful of pocket change, usually meaning I couldn't eat lunch that day. It was rough juggling bills and trying to deem which bill collector was worthy of my hard-earned cash—and who would have to wait an extra week or so. I was constantly working at least two jobs, and in between work I was also going to auditions, taking acting classes, working as an extra, and/or doing commercials--whatever it took to bring in enough money to survive.

It never occurred to me to get on food stamps, although I probably could have qualified. I just worked and worked and worked.

Even back in '96, when I gave up acting, Hollywood was a very different town. There was no such thing as reality shows, no chance at instant fame-for-no-real-reason. No one had computers, digital cameras, or easy access to printers, so maintaining an inventory of updated headshots and résumés was expensive and time-consuming.

Times were tough for me back then, but I cannot imagine how much more difficult it is for young actors in the entertainment industry today. Despite their technological advantages, the almost five dollars per gallon of gas alone would've wiped me out for good, and having to compete with people like Honey Boo Boo for work? Sigh.

Two of my favorite twentysomethings know these difficulties firsthand because they are living the artist's life here in Los Angeles. I'm calling them Sam and Ellie to protect their identities, since both work in very progressive areas of show business and could potentially lose their jobs if I named them.

Sam and Ellie live in an old 1920s apartment building near

downtown Los Angeles. They are within walking distance from some amazing Asian restaurants and know the best places to get interesting and very cheap food, including a rotating sushi bar with "happy hour" sushi at two dollars per plate. They've learned that the cheapest grocery stores are the Mexican and Asian markets, and they save up all their quarters for the local Laundromat.

Like many twentysomethings of the past few decades, they eat lots of ramen noodles (spicy beef is the best) and know every item on every dollar menu in town.

Sam has lived in Los Angeles most of his life. In high school, he was in an award-winning choir with several now-famous movie and TV stars. He was also briefly an actor but instead fell in love with all things behind the scenes, and he is currently working in production with aspirations of being a screenwriter and director. In his spare time, he creates short films and videos, including visuals for Ellie's music.

Ellie is Sam's lovely and ultra-talented girlfriend. She is a musician with a capital *M*. She plays classical guitar, and writes, composes, and produces all her own original music. Ellie has gotten everything she has completely on her own, without any help from big Hollywood manager-types or rich family members.

Despite the fact that Sam and Ellie work in the entertainment industry, they are both conservatives. Their beliefs could literally be a detriment to their line of work, yet they still try to sneak off to listen to Rush Limbaugh and Larry Elder in their cars when they can, and they avoid talking about politics in public. Neither can afford to lose any work in such shaky, unsure times.

I asked what their biggest difficulties are, living in Los Angeles, and both said money.

"It's so hard to keep up," Sam told me, looking down at his hands. "No matter how hard we try, how hard we work, we're still barely getting by."

"If I get some great gig and make a big chunk of money," Ellie said, "by the time we pay our rent and buy food and fill up our cars, it's gone. Completely gone. It's beyond frustrating at times; makes you wonder if it's all worth it."

Sam put an arm around her and added, "Yeah, but I've seen you play crowds of five thousand people, and you see fans that traveled hundreds of miles to hear you sing."

"I know; you're right," Ellie said with a smile. "Yeah, that's when I know I'm doing the right thing."

I also asked them about politics. They are very passionate about their conservative values and equally passionate about what Republicans are doing wrong.

"Young people are fed up with hearing left and right, Democrat and Republican—all of it gets tossed up like a salad and ends up just making you angry and confused," Sam said. "You guys have to find a way to get the message across that this is all about our money. All of it comes down to money, and who exactly is taking our money away from us."

Sam believes that all the conservative-speak about taxes and small government is lost on most young people today. "Talking about their future and how their grandchildren will have to pay is pointless when you don't believe you have a future to look forward to in the first place," he said.

"When I'm in restaurants," he went on, "I talk to the real people—the waiters and busboys—and ask if they're doing better now than they were four years ago. Almost every time, they say no. They tell me about someone in their life, either themselves or their parents or their friends, who are either homeless or jobless and looking for work. This is the worst it's ever been in my life, and I've had a very rough life."

Ellie added, "My friends love Obama. They talk about how

he's going to save us all. They say he's the only politician who's ever cared about them—"

"And that's the problem, right there!" Sam interrupted. "Obama's got *the* message, and it's very, very simple: 'I will help you.' It doesn't matter whether he can actually do it or not, and it doesn't even matter if he's the reason their lives suck—he comes across as the only person who can or will help them. And that's where our side has got to step up. Our side has to find a way to get the message across in simple terms, without a lot of words and rhetoric—that we're the ones who can actually help you, not them. But so far no one's been able to do that."

"The old-school Republicans are what turned so many people our age off," said Ellie. "After the Bush years, people hated Republicans. *Hated* them. They hated anyone that even *looked* like a Republican.

"Sam and I know the difference," she stated with conviction. "We know who the Democrats really are, what they stand for, what they've done. But most kids our age just don't know these things— no one is telling them in a way that makes them listen."

Sam said, "Look at the Occupy Movement and what a screwed-up bunch of people that was—even they couldn't explain what they wanted. They're hearing so many mixed messages, so many lies on TV and in college, and they don't know who or what to believe anymore. And until someone finds a way to get through to them, they're unfortunately the future—and this cycle is going to keep going on and on until there's nothing left of our country."

When Sam and Ellie left, I felt a combination of sadness and hope for them. They have more than most because they have each other; their love exudes all around them. But can they make it in such a crazy, backwards town and in this grim, volatile economy?

As they drove away, I noticed a "Who is John Galt?" bumper sticker on their car. I smiled.

With kids like this in California, I have hope that things are not as lost as they sometimes seem.

11

SPARTAN WARRIOR WOMEN!

by MORGAN BRITTANY

Promise me you'll always remember: You're braver than you believe, and stronger than you seem, and smarter than you think. —A. A. MILNE

This chapter is mainly geared to women, but guys, you can sneak a peek if you want! I feel that we have reached the tipping point in our country. We, as responsible, determined women must step up to the plate as never before. Our conservative, liberty-loving voices need to be heard everywhere. We need to speak up in schools, at work, in PTA meetings, town halls, places of worship, anywhere people can listen to our concerns. Call in to talk shows, write editorials in your local newspaper, and spread the word throughout social media.

Today, regardless of what is said in the media, women hold the key to our future. They are moving into more and more positions of power and wielding more control over the economy. Women make more decisions on home and household purchases, their children's education, and their families' futures than ever before.

Statistics show that even more women today are entering institutes of higher education after high school. They are venturing into fields that were dominated by men as little as ten years ago. Today we see more female computer experts, biologists, graphic artists, and technological experts that we ever have. Many more women are CEOs and CFOs, and they run some of the world's largest companies.

Not only are women advancing more rapidly in the workforce, but many more are successfully combining being a wife, a mother, and a career woman all at the same time. The battle was a lot tougher years ago, before the glass ceiling was broken, but now the floodgates are open, and women are taking the lead in a big way. If you look at just a fraction of the most powerful women in America, this is what you see:

SHERYL SANDBERG, COO, Facebook

VIRGINIA ROMETTY, chairman, president, and CEO, IBM

URSULA BURNS, chairman and CEO, Xerox

MEG WHITMAN, president and CEO, Hewlett Packard

MARISSA MAYER, president and CEO, Yahoo!

ROSALIND BREWER, president and CEO, Sam's Club

PADMASREE WARRIOR, chief technology and strategy officer, Cisco Systems

MARY CALLAHAN ERDOES, CEO, J. P. Morgan, Asset Management division

JANET YELLEN, chair of the Board of Governors, the Federal Reserve

GRETA VAN SUSTEREN, anchor, Fox News

Top businesswomen in the entertainment field, like Oprah Winfrey, Beyoncé, Ellen DeGeneres, and Angelina Jolie, are making strides in all areas, including humanitarian efforts.

Last but definitely not least in the list of most powerful women is the American Mother. This is the woman who chooses the path that is perhaps *the most important* job of all. She may work out of the home; she may not. It is entirely up to her. Some women want to devote full time to their families, while others can manage to combine work and family. Many women have limited options, and the choice is made for them. Perhaps they are single or divorced mothers and need to work to feed their children. Maybe they are going to school to increase their options but still find time to do homework with their kids. Whatever the situation, the earliest role model for a child is a parent, and we all have to bear in mind what a tremendous responsibility that is.

The American Mother is the woman responsible for molding and nurturing the next generation of Americans. She will be the protector who looks out for their education, to make sure the schools are doing their jobs. If a situation comes up, as with "Common Core," Mom will have to know about it, research it, and oppose it if it can potentially hurt her child. This to me is the hardest job in the world, yet there are millions of these unsung heroes out there every day. There are countless stories of successful adults who look back and thank their mother or father for working that extra job just so they could get into college. Yes, it is a sacrifice, but one that we willingly and lovingly make.

Grandmothers, too, watch over and nurture children in many situations. They have a great opportunity to educate and guide them, as well. With their knowledge of the world and their own personal histories, they can teach valuable lessons and life skills. Parents are key to most children's futures, but mothers, fathers, *and* grandparents can all motivate and set examples for the next generation.

Ladies, you are amazing, and I totally believe that there is nothing you can't do. You have strength way beyond what you may think you are capable of. If you look back at the history of our country, women and mothers fought long and hard right alongside the men to ensure our freedom. Maybe they did not go into battle per se, but they were the backbone, the anchor, the voices in the heads of the soldiers on the battlefield. They were the women who sent their husbands, sons, and daughters off to war, knowing that there was a very good chance they might never see them again. Even today, I am in awe of the women who stand so bravely and support their spouses and children in the military, the same women who sometimes receive them back with devastating injuries. Yet, they stand with them, and wouldn't do anything else. They go through their struggles right next to them, holding out that hand that encourages them to try just one more time.

Where does the strength come from? I personally believe that God gives it to us. In my times of crisis, when I feel lost and am having a Scarlett O'Hara moment, I pull myself up off the ground, look up to the sky, and say, "As God is my witness, I'm going to get through this!" We live in difficult times, and all of us put out fires and battle issues in our work and personal lives every day. Of course, we don't have to handle issues that the women of the past had to deal with. We've never had to brave an untamed wilderness, like the original settlers who traveled West against all odds. We were not immersed in the Revolutionary or Civil wars. Perhaps a very small number of women living today experienced the horrors of the Holocaust and life in Nazi Germany, but most of us have no concept of that reality. We face none of the hardships that they did, but in the present day and age, we face different challenges, many of which are just as difficult. We live in a completely different world with circumstances unique to our times. Life is easier for us in some ways, yet enormously more complex in others, but we can all look to our female ancestors, identify with them, and see where our strengths come from.

Every day changes are being made that will affect us and our children. We need to be aware of what is happening and what legislation is being passed for good or bad. We do not live in a world where we can just *assume* that the right things are being done on our behalf. Unfortunately, dangerous and destructive things are being done to undermine our country, and unless we keep our radar up, laws and regulations that you may not even want will be enacted. At least if you are aware and voice an opinion in favor or against an issue, legislators won't be able to quietly slide it through. This is why we need some of you courageous women to step forward to the front lines.

Politically, women are growing their numbers. Just think back a little over thirty years ago. At that time there were only two females in the Senate, nineteen in the House of Representatives, and one on the Supreme Court. By 2013 there were twenty in the Senate, seventy-nine in the House, and three on the Supreme Court. There are also twenty-nine female US ambassadors. We now have five women governors running states in this country. Among them are Susana Martinez (R-NM), Jan Brewer (R-AZ), Mary Fallin (R-OK), and Nikki Haley (R-SC). With any luck we will add to that in the coming elections. We can do it, and we must.

We need to run for positions of political power. I mean everything. City council, school board, mayor, state assembly, state senate, state representative—the sky is the limit. Hey, let's go for president! What a dream it would be to see one of our strong, principled, "take no prisoners" conservative women run against Hillary Clinton in 2016! Can you imagine the excitement of a presidential race between two women? I would love to see how the media would handle that! They couldn't use the gender card, and probably wouldn't drag them through the mud as much as they did Sarah Palin for fear of a backlash. Because of their political correctness, the media would have to change their strategy, and I would love to see it. It certainly would get people engaged in the political system once again. We need that strong woman to step forward and run, win, and set things straight in Washington, DC!

So, the leftists in this country want to take away our ammo? Let's take away *theirs*! If we can load up our side with more and more amazing women and find one to run for president, they won't be able to use the "war on women" mantra anymore. Let *them* trivialize women and only talk about how much the government can do for them. Let *them* label women as victims because no one wants to pay for their birth control or abortions. Let *them* whine about how women don't receive equal opportunity and equal pay. *We don't whine!* We don't look for handouts and entitlements from the government. Let Julia, from Barack Obama's "Life of Julia" video, be their representative woman. We will take Lady Liberty!

There would be a sharp contrast between Hillary Clinton and any conservative woman candidate. I think for the first time there would be a clear picture of who she is and who we are. The waters wouldn't be muddied as they have been in the past few presidential elections, with our side trying to be Democrat "Lite." It hasn't worked, and now is the right time for a game change. We need clear, concise, bold ideas coming from a strong lady. Other countries have done it. Why not us?

Every one of you reading this has a talent you can offer to further our cause. PolitiChicks started as the germ of an idea that grew and then exploded in popularity. No matter what your talent or skill, we need you. We need you to start the chain of strength that gets stronger as each link is added.

We all know deep down in the depths of our souls that if we don't stand up right now, our children and grandchildren will be living in a country that we won't even recognize. I barely recognize it now, and every day I feel as though I am running faster and faster just trying to keep up with the stones and arrows coming at my country.

I know it is difficult to take on the opposition and try to beat them back. You can be sure that you will be criticized, ridiculed, called names, and possibly even ostracized by some of your friends, but this is crunch time, and there is no room to be hesitant or weak.

I, like Ann-Marie and Dr. Gina, have been heckled at Tea Party rallies, threatened on social media sites, and written about in the vilest ways. Sure, it hurts at first, but then you start to just tune the haters out and go on with your mission. As an actress, I can't even begin to tell you how many rotten reviews I have gotten in my day! Had I paid any real attention to them, I would have just packed up and gone home.

Probably no conservative woman has taken more flak than Sarah Palin. Like her or not, you have to admire her unwavering fight for this country and our principals. The left was out in full force from the moment she exploded onto the scene. Their goal was to take her down, but they found out it wasn't so easy. She has taken attacks on her looks, her speech, her intelligence, and her background, and the cruelest arrows were aimed at her children. Her "Mama Grizzly" attitude took over when they pushed her too far, and she roared back. She is a loud, strong voice and a thorn in the side of the left. I liken her to John Wayne in *True Grit,* and I can almost hear her saying to the libs when there is a standoff, "Fill your hand, you son of a b***h!" We, like Sarah, need to lift up our shields, ask God for strength, and forge ahead, because we are not alone.

There are millions of us out there, in every walk of life, in every age group. Our values are just as valid as those being pushed on us from the other side. Those of us who are older must teach younger women to stay true to their values and what they believe in. One of the most difficult things in this world is to go against the tide and current public opinion. We must teach our younger sisters to stand strong and speak out for what they believe. If they know that there are large numbers of us, it makes it easier. Not easy . . . but easier.

Yes, we have an uphill battle, but let's not look at the mountain before us; let's look up just far enough to take those first few steps. The first steps up the mountain are sometimes the hardest because it takes courage to actually start the climb. If we approach this challenge knowing that every step we take is getting us closer to our goal, we can win back the America of our Founders.

It's all right to start small. I am probably preaching to the choir, because if you are reading this book, you are already a concerned patriot. Maybe you can pass along some of these suggestions next time you take a progressive to lunch!

Let's begin by educating our children about the greatness of this country. The schools do a great job of tearing it down; the colleges indoctrinate our youth into believing that America is a mean country, so we must counteract that. Think how many hours a day the schools have your children. You need to at least open a dialogue for a few minutes every day to find out what they are absorbing for those many hours. With busy schedules it sometimes slips through the cracks, and we let too much time go by without being aware of what our children are being taught, but now it is of primary importance. With Common Core being foisted upon us, we need to be vigilant.

Sit down with your kids and show them great films and television celebrating the heroes and the goodness of who we are as a nation. Depending on their age, watch *Saving Private Ryan* and *The Patriot*. Continue with *Forrest Gump, Glory, Lincoln*, and *Mr. Smith Goes to Washington*. *United 93* is particularly important because it is a more current event. And if you want some all-out fun, show them *Top Gun*, and I guarantee some little boy will want to be a fighter pilot. (You see what I mean in chapter 9 about Hollywood being capable of producing positive product?) Take the opportunity to read to them about the great heroes of our country, both past and present. There are many good books out there that are entertaining to all ages, most recently Rush Limbaugh's children's books.

Celebrate with your families, and don't let the real meaning of patriotic and religious holidays get lost. Every year there seems to be a battle over nativity scenes and Christmas trees or other religious themes. If your city or town tries to stomp on your holiday, gather up a group of people, call the local TV and radio stations, and take a stand! Most of these politically correct persecutors will back down if you shine the light on them. Look at the groups who get the most attention; they make the most noise! We can do it in a nonhostile, dignified way. We can disarm our foes and use humor as Ronald Reagan did. We don't need to show hatred, anger, and intolerance, like the left; we can debate and win on the facts.

Just remember: there are more of us than there are of them. Try as they will, the media will continue to make you think that you are in the minority and the world is progressing and shifting away from conservatism. NOT TRUE. They have been feeding us that stale story for years, and unfortunately, people buy into it. Travel with me sometime to the heartland, to the North, the South, and all the way to Alaska, and your heart will be warmed to know that we have the numbers.

The radical progressive left thinks we are stupid and weak. They think that we won't fight back. Sometimes I feel that way, too, when

I look at our leaders in Congress. It frustrates me when they just roll over and give up or compromise on issues that will mold our future. We need grit and guts to win this battle; it is not for the timid. If your representatives are not working for you or not listening to what you say . . . vote them out or run for their seats! Call them and tell them that is what you intend to do.

Too many in Washington believe that we work for them. Newsflash! They work for *us!* They shouldn't have cushy jobs with dozens of perks and do what *they* want. They need to do what *we* want, and that will start the ball rolling to a better America.

All right, ladies, let's lock and load. No matter what we do in the fight, whether it is big or small, we can all be proud to say that we stood up, made our voices heard, saved our families, and defended America!

As we head out, remember the words of the great Lt. Gen. Lewis Burwell "Chesty" Puller, the most decorated US Marine in history. At the Battle of Chosin Reservoir, one of the nastiest conflicts of the Korean War, when his troops were surrounded by the Chinese military, Puller cried, "They're on our right, they're on our left, they're in front of us and they're behind us; they can't get away from us this time!"

12

TWENTY YEARS FROM TODAY

by GINA LOUDON

It's never too late to do the right thing. That's what I'll do, I'll go over there and do the right thing.[1] —NICK MARSHALL, *WHAT WOMEN WANT*

I start books by reading the last chapter. So if this is where you started your exploration of *What Women* Really *Want,* then you are in good company. Well, you are at least in my company! So I am glad to have you here.

There's a method to our madness. I start at the end because I figure the end is where the author's advice is, and if the author's advice to me is not worth it, then I don't need to read the book.

My approach to life is similar. I start with a well-defined goal, and work backward, in timeline fashion. I do this for fun, for my career goals, for my marriage, for my charity work, and for my children.

TELEVISION SCREENS

Before 9/11, my goal for my life was clean. I was the wife of a successful politician who won elections with seeming ease, and I felt honor in my role as his key supporter and trusted advisor. I was the sidekick, a right-hand woman, or helpmeet, as I liked to think of it. I loved that role. I enjoyed getting to be on the inside of all he was doing—helping, watching, and recruiting to make it all happen for him. I wanted no part of the limelight but just loved standing by my man. I thought it would always be that way. I fantasized that after he served his terms, he would get into the private sector so we could enjoy our lives more, and travel, and live more dreams.

I wanted to raise smart children who were equipped to take the world by storm and make it better. In my mind, that meant that I was somehow excused from the drudgery and ugliness of career, politics, and civic activism. My role in my children's lives would be that of a stay-at-home, homeschooling mama, and I wore the title proudly. I wanted to use my degrees to write articles and marketing plans, to promote worthy projects on a voluntary basis, and to do charity work. I wanted to be a good friend to people I liked, and I didn't want to have to deal with conflict or confrontation or trying to love those who were hard to love. My children, my husband, my career, and my friendships were tied up neatly and securely, and I had my mental plan. I looked at the women in politics scratching and clawing each other to try to succeed, and I knew I wanted no part of that!

Then one morning on our way to the Capitol building to begin our week in my husband's Senate office, some terrorists changed that for me.

John and I had just returned from a trip to New York with other senators and their wives, where I remember staring out the top floor of the NBC building, toward our hotel, where our children were staying with a nanny in a top-floor room. I could see our exact suite, where I knew our children were playing, as I gazed out over the rim of my first-ever twenty-five-dollar margarita. And I had the strangest thought. I wondered what would happen if there were an emergency of some sort. I contemplated how I would get to my children. *If I could fly like a bird*, I remember thinking, *I could get to them in no time.* The buildings were so close. But knowing that it would take me an hour to get to them on foot made me uneasy.

These thoughts troubled me over and over for the next week. That was August 2001. Later, on my way back to the Midwest, I learned that I was pregnant with our first boy. Now there would be one *more* child to think about in an emergency.

SCRAMBLED EGGS AND SCRAMBLED THOUGHTS

The morning of September 11 was beautiful. I awoke to birds singing, and I remember opening all the windows to let in the day before flipping on the news to get my bearings for the week. I stepped out on our balcony and noticed the clear, blue sky. I was excited for the week ahead. I usually took our children and went with John to his Senate office in the Capitol, so I could help in his office and be nearby in case he needed me. I wrote press releases, helped sort constituent mail, greeted guests who came to see him, and even gave tours of the Capitol to those who wanted to go.

Instantly, I knew this day would be different.

The South Tower of the World Trade Center, which we had just seen on our trip to New York, was smoking. As I listened to the details on the television, I took a step back and sat down on the bed, knowing that life from that moment on would be different.

As I watched the demonic details of that morning unfold, I frantically called John from the kitchen, where he was making breakfast. I wanted him by my side. We exchanged glances as the severity of what we were witnessing took hold. Then we held each other.

John and I kept glancing at one another, and then back at the horror displayed on our television screen. We knew we needed to leave for the Capitol, but I just wanted to duck and cover.

The two-hour drive to the Capitol was chilling. We heard that two buildings were hit, then the Pentagon, and a plane had gone down in Pennsylvania. There was talk that the White House had been targeted. We wondered if the world was ending.

With the children strapped safely in their car seats, we turned up the back speakers and rocked their music so they couldn't hear what we were hearing.

John said he preferred that the children and I go to a nearby hotel. Security was thick the closer we got to the Capitol, and we didn't know what the enemy was going to target next. I told John that if the world was going to end, I wanted to keep my family together. John conceded.

That day bookmarked the beginning of a new normal for America, and my family was no exception. I remembered my recent trip to New York City and how I'd looked out one skyscraper to another, where my children were. I never wanted to go back. I was haunted with nightmares about those towers, and the towers that had separated my children from us only weeks before. Everything changed that day. Some changes were for the better. Some changes for the worse. Some changes are harder to gauge.

ASHES

My entire vision for my life, and that of my country and my family, had changed. I began to see my role as rather insignificant in the light of what had happened to our world that day. And I began to dig my way out of the ashes of my mind to ask God what He would have me do.

Not long after that, I heard about a woman named Kitty

Werthmann, a Holocaust survivor–turned Tea Partier. Kitty is an ardent advocate for the Bill of Rights. She gave a powerful speech in 2010 in which she spoke about the dangers of not standing up to political tyrants. She had watched her country of Austria rather quickly—in a span of five years—go from a free and religious society to one where guns were confiscated and crucifixes were replaced with photographs of Herr Hitler. But it wasn't by force. "We elected him by a landslide 98% of the vote," she said.[2]

Austria was in a depression, and the Communists and Socialists were fighting for control. "We were promised that a vote for Hitler would mean the end of unemployment and help for the family," Werthmann recalled. Within a few weeks after Germany annexed Austria, everyone was employed. Then things started to change:

"Our education was nationalized. . . . Our teacher, a very devout woman, stood up and told the class we wouldn't pray or have religion anymore. Instead, we sang 'Deutschland, Deutschland, Uber Alles,' and had physical education."

Werthmann also talked about the dangers of welfare and a nationalized health care system and how they can lead to militancy. When the war started, food was rationed and "a full-employment law was passed which meant if you didn't work, you didn't get a ration card, and if you didn't have a card, you starved to death."

According to Werthmann, Austrians received high-quality health care before Hitler, but after he nationalized health care, people started going to the doctor for everything. "There was no money for research as it was poured into socialized medicine," she said. "Research at the medical schools literally stopped, so the best doctors left Austria and emigrated to other countries . . . [and] our tax rates went up to 80% of our income." Werthmann went on to describe how, when she was a student teacher in the Alps, the government came to take the few mentally challenged people in the village to a "training center" in Germany. The officials promised those taken would return in six months, and would know how to read and write, but soon the villagers received letters saying their relatives had mysteriously died of natural causes.

Werthmann told about how her brother-in-law, who owned a restaurant, was harassed by government officials. They told him he needed to replace his square tables with round ones so people wouldn't get hurt, and that he had to add another bathroom. The regulations put him out of business.

"Next came gun registration," Werthmann said. Because of "gun violence," first citizens had everyone register their guns. Then police just flat-out confiscated them. The erosion of rights came over a five-year period. "Had it happened overnight, my countrymen would have fought to the last breath. Instead, we had creeping gradualism," she said.

I had visited the home of Anne Frank, seen the ravages of the Holocaust in East Germany, and even prayed in Red Square for our country. But what could I really do to prevent a repeat of any of the above in America? I was just one mom with a little tribe of children entrusted to me and no clue how to fix the world, with all of its problems.

I watched it get worse.

It was beginning to look as though being a mom and raising up my little army might not be enough. And perhaps, using my degrees to write an occasional marketing plan was vanity. It appeared that God was calling me—calling a mother.

My husband's Senate term was ending, and I began to believe that God must want me to run. I knew John had been an exemplary senator, and I wanted to continue that tradition for the good constituents who elected him and loved him so. I told God my plans.

THE BEST-LAID PLANS

When I ran for my husband's Senate seat, sure that I was called and would win, I lost. God was probably smiling that day, as parents do when they know good is just around the corner for their children. But I certainly wasn't laughing. Confusion set in.

I recalled a conversation I'd had with John when we had discussed our children's potential career paths.

John had a large chess set he had purchased on a trip to Mexico. He kept it in his Senate office, and many late nights were enjoyed by friends, family, visitors, and other senators and staffers playing chess. John always kept a cutout of his face taped over the front of one of the pawns. People laughed at this, but John explained to my children and me that when it all shook out, he was just a pawn. Even sitting in his elaborately appointed Senate office, that of a senior senator, overlooking the Missouri river, the Governor's mansion, the eagles nesting, and the beautiful fountains, he saw himself as a pawn. He wanted to be used, and he recognized that the real power was never in the hands of the politicians, anyway.

"The real power," he said, "is in the power of the pen." The press had the real power to change things. They got to define the narrative, to write the story, to take down whom they deemed worthless, and even to prop up whom they deemed worthy. The power of the pen was undeniably impressive.

But I wasn't looking for power for the sake of power. I was looking for the power to save my children's future.

I cried as I poured out my heart to John. First, I told him there was no way I could be in the press. I mean, why would they want someone who had too many degrees from progressive universities to talk about conservative politics? Who would listen?

John reminded me that I had done interviews for him, and that I had handled the press releases and even writing of many different campaigns. He reminded me of the long hours writing two theses and a doctoral dissertation that had earned high honors in schools where the odds were against me, as a conservative. I had fought, and lost, and was still fighting, he said, and God would honor that.

Then he quoted to me the words of Teddy Roosevelt:

> It is not the critic who counts; not the man who points out how the strong man stumbles, or where the doer of deeds could have done them better. The credit belongs to the man who is actually in the arena, whose face is marred by dust and sweat and blood; who strives valiantly; who errs, who comes short again and again, because there is no effort without error and shortcoming; but who does actually strive to do the deeds; who knows great enthusiasms, the great devotions; who spends himself in a worthy cause; who at the best knows in the end the triumph of high achievement, and who at the worst, if he fails, at least fails while daring greatly, so that his place shall never be with those cold and timid souls who neither know victory nor defeat.[3]

I still wasn't sure.

I began to test the waters, starting my own blog and volunteering to write for my friend Andrew Breitbart's blog. I traveled a little to speak, and I was gaining some real traction in churches, moms' groups, and graduations as a speaker. I was becoming a regular guest on radio shows, and soon after, television shows, as well. I began to hear my message clearly, and I knew God was honoring my diligence, in spite of my numerous failures and weaknesses.

Within the year, after saying I never wanted to go back to New York, I was doing so regularly, appearing on Fox News and Fox Business and writing for various national outlets, and I was offered my own radio show on a small station in Missouri, where I would later be promoted to the evening drive host on a superstation in the heart of the South, Birmingham, Alabama.

As fate would have it, I later got to interview Kitty Werthmann, the Holocaust survivor, on my radio show, and was even more struck by her story. I wondered if Austrians had been any different from New Yorkers when terror struck in their homeland.

It is odd to me that immediately after 9/11, citizens became so spiritual, so moral—for a moment. How could culture change so quickly from that moment? Maybe our hearts hardened. Perhaps we became complacent as a way to avoid the strong emotions we felt. Maybe we just wanted to look away as a nation. Maybe that is the reason our culture seemed to decline from godly to ungodly, from thankful to ungrateful, from aware to oblivious, in a matter of a few years.

HAUNTED

That year, still hoping to stay under the radar and off the stage, I helped coordinate an event for ten thousand people at Kiener Plaza, protesting the government takeover of America's health care system. I knew that with that single government conquest, 20 percent of the American economy would be socialized. I saw the similarities between Kitty Werthmann's Austria and my America. At the event, a law student I knew set up a gulag to show the extreme of statism.

Until then, even though we saw our country going the wrong direction, I don't think I had ever really stopped to contemplate how far down the wrong road we had gone. But at that moment, the reality hit me. We were so far down the road to totalitarianism that I wasn't sure I saw a road back. There I was, a speaker in front of ten thousand people, and all I could see was that gulag. I had traveled extensively in eastern Europe but had never been so haunted by anything I had seen. I reasoned that it must be a combination of my fear for our country and what I knew about history and statism. Like so many other times in my life, I wished I didn't know what

I knew. In the movie *Matrix*, Neo was faced with two choices: the blue pill, which would keep him in the world of illusion, and the red pill, which would allow him to live free in the world of truth. I had swallowed the red pill.

ONE QUESTION

A question began to burn inside of me, one question that haunted me, like my tower dreams from 9/11. The thought surpassed all others: *What did Kitty Werthmann's mother do to prevent the horrors of the Holocaust generation?*

From that point on, my nights became an obsessive avoidance of falling asleep, for fear of dreaming. But sleep came anyway, and with it, the nightmares.

I dreamed of being slowly escorted, with my ankles chained, into a dark, musty gulag. A hard-looking female warden, who had me by my arm, sat me down across from my daughter at the end of the long, dark hallway. My heart dropped as I looked over to see that my child was there, too. She looked gaunt and filthy, and her tearstained face was vacant, expressionless. I wanted to grab her and cradle her safely in my arms, but for some unknown reason, I knew that if I did, it could pose a danger to us. As the others started to mumble to one another, she looked up from her despair and said to me, "Mama, what did you do to prevent this?"

I woke with a start, and my mind began searching for answers to the question she'd asked before I woke from my personal hell.

I had this dream over and over, and then I would be haunted and tense the next day.

My daughter's question echoed in my mind. I had so many answers, I thought: "I took you to church and to ballet and to piano, and I schooled you and I disciplined you and I loved you, and I nursed you and I taught you the Bible and I loved your daddy, and

I made a happy home, and we baked pies and we decorated for Christmas, and we sang and laughed and played, and I was your mama, and I wanted to make you a warrior!"

But then reality hit me like a bullet in the gut: She didn't need me to make her a warrior. In my nightmare, that wouldn't have helped anyway, and we both knew it. She needed me to *be* her warrior.

The dream that haunted me had immense power over me. It caused me to act out of fear for months. I became frustrated enough in my helplessness to take myself on as a patient, and to think about what I would tell a client in my psychological care, who was having the same dreams. I realized that my power was in my action, and I knew I had to fight back, both in my dream and in my life.

I knew what to do. That night, I confronted my demon.

THE EXORCISM

Again, I found myself walking down a dark, dank hallway of the same concrete gulag. A female warden escorted me and seated me on a concrete ledge. I expected to see my daughter across from me, but this time, she wasn't there. Where was she? My mind set to panic, and I felt my heart race. I could hear its thump in my chest, and a chill went up my spine.

A nice, gray-haired lady approached me and asked me to come with her. She held my elbow gently. Instead of the stark, white uniform of the usual warden I saw, this lady was in gray, or maybe blue, with a proper white, scalloped collar. She wore nylons and black grandma shoes. I felt comforted.

She took me to a room in another part of the complex, and at the front of the room was an old television, the kind with the scratchy "bug races" buzzing across the screen. Without saying a word, she nodded at me and gave me a slight grin, as if to tell me to be patient.

I wasn't patient! I wanted to know where my daughter was!

The TV scratched to a flash, and then a family was shown on-screen. It took me a moment to digest, but I realized it was my family. I saw my children filing into our car, and we were going somewhere. John was loading campaign signs for some other candidate, and we looked happy and busy.

Then the TV went to scratchy again.

In only moments, though, I saw a frame of my family walking neighborhoods, handing out literature. I couldn't see who it was for, but it bore flags and stars in red, white, and blue. The only color I could see was on those stars and stripes, but I felt unbelievable comfort in that.

The TV screen flashed again. This time, it was a video of me, arguing with someone on a national television program. I could tell by watching my body language that I was fighting with all I had. My passion was evident, and my conviction was glaring. I couldn't tell if I was winning the argument or not, but I certainly was holding my own.

Suddenly, faces flashed across the screen. I am still uncertain why, but I recognized some and not others.

I became startled as I saw the shadow of a person with a gun. It was a large gun, but the figure was small. As the television went in and out of focus, I could see that the figure was a woman . . . It was *me*! And I was firing at a target and hitting every time.

As I continued to watch the target, however, I realized that it was *not* me after all, but my daughter. Confused, but glad to see her shooting prowess, I began to think she was somehow safe.

But the screen began flashing again, with shots of me on a stage, me at a microphone, me writing a book, me at a party platform meeting, me leading a strategy session, and other things I can't recall. Then the screen went black.

It held that blackness for what seemed like several minutes, and then at last, I saw my daughter's face again.

She looked pretty, happy, healthy. But still, she asked me the dreaded question: "Mama," she said, "what were you doing when our country was being overtaken?"

I looked at the screen, scraping to find my shaky voice. It wouldn't come. "I . . . I was fighting," I answered. But I sounded like a dying seal, or something. I stiffened my arms and took a breath. "I was fighting like hell!" I screamed. "Didn't you see that?"

I definitely had my voice now! "I gave everything I had, and I fought. Every day I fought! I never shied away from an arena. I fought every moment I was given the chance. I taught you to fight, too, and your siblings. And we fought together! I left the comfort and security of our happy life to fight for you. I gave it all I had!"

I felt the gentle touch of my escort, and realized her fingers were warm. Then I looked at my daughter, crying in despair. I had to let my daughter know that I fought . . .

The warden smiled warmly, still not saying a word, but her nod in the direction of the old television told me that the movie was not over.

I looked at the TV again, desperately trying to wipe the tears away and calm my breathing so I could see and hear. There was my daughter's face again . . .

"Mama, I know, and I want you to know that I thank you, and that I am fine, and we will be fine, because you fought."

I gasped and looked over to find my escort gone, and the hard coldness of the gulag was gone too. I realized that I was safe in my bed, staring at the ceiling, comforted by the steady breathing of my husband next to me.

I ran into my children's rooms and checked everyone. All were safe and sleeping. I sat at the edge of my daughter's bed, stroking her hair and trying to get ahold of my tears. And I comforted myself, realizing that I had beaten the demon, and that the dream would probably not recur now.

But what would have happened if my daughter had *not* told me she was okay? What if we were still there, in that horrible gulag, and I had to answer her question? What then?

That is when I put the final knife in the face of that demon. I knew the answer.

I knew that if I ever had to sit across from my child in that horrible situation, at least I would be able to look her in the eye and say, "I fought like hell. I stopped at nothing. I surrendered all pride, all comfort, to fight for your future with all I had. And though we stopped from time to time to enjoy our lives, we focused on truth, and we waged war on the enemy!"

That moment, my sense of personal meaning changed.

I got my license to carry a gun, and I vowed to take every opportunity given me to speak the truth. I vowed to take extra time to listen to those who disagree with me, to challenge my ideas. I vowed to bring my children with me whenever I could, so they would see the behaviors I wanted them to learn, in case they would need them one day, and so we could stay together.

I vowed to fight for the only contract the American people have to defend them against tyranny: the US Constitution, and the Bill of Rights in particular. I vowed to fight for the only contract that the grassroots have with the people they elect, the Party Platform, and the planks that speak to the culture, especially. And I vowed to tell as many people as I could that the planks in the GOP platform encompass every value necessary to keep our children safe, our homes secure, and our country free, if only we hold our politicians to it.

I vowed to take down the elitists in both parties who think they are above their contract with the people who hired them, and to work for those who are willing to fight for freedom. I vowed to write books and give speeches, to take risks every day, and to be fearless. I vowed to love those who annoy me, to defend those who cannot defend themselves, to be bigger than those who tried to pull me down (and to give them even better reasons to hate me). I vowed to pull those I envy onto my team, because if I envy them, that means they have something I wish I had. We are more powerful united. I vowed to discard those who backstab, stir up strife, and create drama. I vowed to win.

I vowed to laugh—and to be willing to be laughed at. I vowed to be strong and to be vulnerable. I vowed to know more than my opponents, even though I hate that.

That moment, I became the mother, the wife, the friend, and the patriot I knew God intended me to be. I was a mama grizzly, ready to fight for her cubs. I was a defender of truth, willing to share the facts. I was an emboldened warrior, who would stop at nothing to defend those she loved. I was a warrior surrendered to an almighty, loving God, who holds the world in His hands. And I was an optimist, because I had seen the end of the story, and I knew my role. I was all I wanted to be.

In that moment, I tasted freedom, and I was thankful. That was all I'd ever wanted.

I think that is what all women want.

At the beginning of the book, Ann-Marie talks about her divorce from the left wing of American politics. But have we thought about our marriage, our commitment to the patriot movement?

It's important to challenge your own ability to defend the truth, but have you vowed to listen to those who disagree with you? Take time to listen, too.

Have you vowed to defend the US Constitution, the Bill of Rights, and the most conservative party platform before they are too weak to defend you?

Have you vowed to take down the elite in DC in BOTH parties?

Have you vowed to be fearless? To take a risk every day? I love the adage "Do right and fear no man." Fear is an utter waste of time. Take risks. Know your strengths and rock them!

Have you vowed to put the movement over fame and personal aspirations, and put enemy fire over friendly fire? That is when we start winning again. Criticize the other side all you want, but they are masters of this concept. When is the last time you heard a statist criticize a statist? Vow to discard those who backstab, stir up strife, and create drama. Every general knows that confusion in the camp results in loss. We have no time left to lose. Have you vowed to win?

Have you vowed to laugh? And be willing to be laughed at? Have you vowed to be strong and be vulnerable? To know more than your opponents?

Have you vowed to taste freedom every day so that you can remember why you are fighting. Do you remind yourself every day that victory is within your grasp?

Finally, because it is most important, please do the following:

WRITE A LETTER TO YOUR CHILD

I. Write a manifesto, a promise, or just a plan of action to your child.

II. Write about your relationship with your child/children, and what it means to you.

III. Write about your hopes for their future, their lives, their freedom.

We are the land of the Free and the Home of the *brave*. I almost always sign my books that we are only *free* because we are *brave*. Never forget that. Stay brave.

APPENDIX A

THE DECLARATION OF INDEPENDENCE

IN CONGRESS, JULY 4, 1776.

The unanimous Declaration of the thirteen united States of America, When in the Course of human events, it becomes necessary for one people to dissolve the political bands which have connected them with another, and to assume among the powers of the earth, the separate and equal station to which the Laws of Nature and of Nature's God entitle them, a decent respect to the opinions of mankind requires that they should declare the causes which impel them to the separation.

We hold these truths to be self-evident, that all men are created equal, that they are endowed by their Creator with certain unalienable Rights, that among these are Life, Liberty and the pursuit of Happiness.--That to secure these rights, Governments are instituted among Men, deriving their just powers from the consent of the governed, --That whenever any Form of Government becomes destructive of these ends, it is the Right of the People to alter or to abolish it, and to institute new Government, laying its foundation on such principles and organizing its powers in such form, as to them shall seem most likely to effect their Safety and Happiness. Prudence, indeed, will dictate that Governments long established should not be changed for light and transient causes; and accordingly all experience hath shewn, that mankind are more disposed to suffer, while evils are sufferable, than to right themselves by abolishing the forms to which they are accustomed. But when a long train of abuses and usurpations, pursuing invariably the same Object evinces a design to reduce them under absolute Despotism, it is their right, it is their duty, to throw off such Government, and to provide new Guards for their future security.--Such has been the patient sufferance of these Colonies; and such is now the necessity which constrains them to alter their former Systems of Government. The history of the present King of Great Britain is a history of repeated injuries and usurpations, all having in direct object the establishment of an absolute Tyranny over these States. To prove this, let Facts be submitted to a candid world.

He has refused his Assent to Laws, the most wholesome and necessary for the public good. He has forbidden his Governors to pass Laws of immediate and pressing importance, unless suspended in their operation till his Assent should be obtained; and when so suspended, he has utterly neglected to attend to them. He has refused to pass other Laws for the accommodation of large districts of people, unless those people would relinquish the right of Representation in the Legislature, a right inestimable to them and formidable to tyrants only. He has called together legislative bodies at places unusual, uncomfortable, and distant from the depository of their public Records, for the sole purpose of fatiguing them into compliance with his measures. He has dissolved Representative Houses repeatedly, for opposing with manly firmness his invasions on the rights of the people. He has refused for a long time, after such dissolutions, to cause others to be elected; whereby the Legislative powers, incapable of Annihilation, have returned to the People at large for their exercise; the State remaining in the mean time exposed to all the dangers of invasion from without, and convulsions within. He has endeavoured to prevent the population of these States; for that purpose obstructing the Laws for Naturalization of Foreigners; refusing to pass others to encourage their migrations hither, and raising the conditions of new Appropriations of Lands. He has obstructed the Administration of Justice, by refusing his Assent to Laws for establishing Judiciary powers. He has made Judges dependent on his Will alone, for the tenure of their offices, and the amount and payment of their salaries. He has erected a multitude of New Offices, and sent hither swarms of Officers to harrass our people, and eat out their substance. He has kept among us, in times of peace, Standing Armies without the Consent of our legislatures. He has affected to render the Military independent of and superior to the Civil power. He has combined with others to subject us to a jurisdiction foreign to our constitution, and unacknowledged by our laws; giving his Assent to their Acts of pretended Legislation: For Quartering large bodies of armed troops among us: For protecting them, by a mock Trial, from punishment for any Murders which they should commit on the Inhabitants of these States: For cutting off our Trade with all parts of the world: For imposing Taxes on us without our Consent: For depriving us in many cases, of the benefits of Trial by Jury: For transporting us beyond Seas to be tried for pretended offences For abolishing the free System of English Laws in a neighbouring Province, establishing therein an Arbitrary government, and enlarging its Boundaries so as to render it at once an example and fit instrument for introducing the same absolute rule into these Colonies: For taking away our Charters, abolishing our most valuable Laws, and altering fundamentally the Forms of our Governments: For suspending our own Legislatures, and declaring themselves invested with power to legislate for us in all cases whatsoever. He has abdicated Government here, by declaring us out of his Protection and waging War against us. He has plundered our seas, ravaged our Coasts, burnt our towns, and destroyed the lives of our people. He is at this time transporting large Armies of foreign Mercenaries to compleat the works of death, desolation and tyranny, already begun with circumstances of Cruelty & perfidy scarcely paralleled in the most barbarous ages, and totally unworthy the Head of a civilized nation. He has constrained our fellow Citizens taken Captive on the high Seas to bear Arms against their Country, to become the executioners of their friends and Brethren, or to fall themselves by their Hands. He has excited domestic insurrections amongst us, and has endeavoured to bring on the inhabitants of our frontiers, the merciless Indian Savages, whose known rule of warfare, is an undistinguished destruction of all ages, sexes and conditions.

In every stage of these Oppressions We have Petitioned for Redress in the most humble terms: Our repeated Petitions have been answered only by repeated injury. A Prince whose character is thus marked by every act which may define a Tyrant, is unfit to be the ruler of a free people.

Nor have We been wanting in attentions to our Brittish brethren. We have warned them from time to time of attempts by their legislature to extend an unwarrantable jurisdiction over us. We have reminded them of the circumstances of our emigration and settlement here. We have appealed to their native justice and magnanimity, and we have conjured them by the ties of our common kindred to disavow these usurpations, which, would inevitably interrupt our connections and correspondence. They too have been deaf to the voice of justice and of consanguinity. We must, therefore, acquiesce in the necessity, which denounces our Separation, and hold them, as we hold the rest of mankind, Enemies in War, in Peace Friends.

We, therefore, the Representatives of the united States of America, in General Congress, Assembled, appealing to the Supreme Judge of the world for the rectitude of our intentions, do, in the Name, and by Authority of the good People of these Colonies, solemnly publish and declare, That these United Colonies are, and of Right ought to be Free and Independent States; that they are Absolved from all Allegiance to the British Crown, and that all political connection between them and the State of Great Britain, is and ought to be totally dissolved; and that as Free and Independent States, they have full Power to levy War, conclude Peace, contract Alliances, establish Commerce, and to do all other Acts and Things which Independent States may of right do. And for the support of this Declaration, with a firm reliance on the protection of divine Providence, we mutually pledge to each other our Lives, our Fortunes and our sacred Honor.

THE 56 SIGNATURES APPEAR IN THE POSITIONS INDICATED:

GEORGIA: Button Gwinnett   Lyman Hall   George Walton

NORTH CAROLINA: William Hooper   Joseph Hewes   John Penn
SOUTH CAROLINA: Edward Rutledge   Thomas Heyward, Jr.
Thomas Lynch, Jr.   Arthur Middleton

MASSACHUSETTS: John Hancock
MARYLAND: Samuel Chase   William Paca   Thomas Stone
Charles Carroll of Carrollton
VIRGINIA: George Wythe Richard Henry Lee Thomas Jefferson
Benjamin Harrison   Thomas Nelson, Jr.   Francis Lightfoot
Lee Carter Braxton

PENNSYLVANIA: Robert Morris   Benjamin Rush   Benjamin
Franklin John Morton George Clymer James Smith George
Taylor   James Wilson   George Ross
DELAWARE: Caesar Rodney   George Read   Thomas McKean

NEW YORK: William Floyd   Philip Livingston   Francis Lewis
Lewis Morris
NEW JERSEY: Richard Stockton   John Witherspoon   Francis
Hopkinson   John Hart   Abraham Clark

NEW HAMPSHIRE: Josiah Bartlett   William Whipple
Massachusetts: Samuel Adams   John Adams   Robert Treat Paine
Elbridge Gerry
RHODE ISLAND: Stephen Hopkins   William Ellery
CONNECTICUT: Roger Sherman   Samuel Huntington   William
Williams   Oliver Wolcott
NEW HAMPSHIRE: Matthew Thornton

APPENDIX B

THE BILL OF RIGHTS

THE PREAMBLE TO THE BILL OF RIGHTS

Congress of the United States begun and held at the City of New-York, on Wednesday the fourth of March, one thousand seven hundred and eighty nine.

The Conventions of a number of the States, having at the time of their adopting the Constitution, expressed a desire, in order to prevent misconstruction or abuse of its powers, that further declaratory and restrictive clauses should be added: And as extending the ground of public confidence in the Government, will best ensure the beneficent ends of its institution.

Resolved by the Senate and House of Representatives of the United States of America, in Congress assembled, two thirds of both Houses concurring, that the following Articles be proposed to the Legislatures of the several States, as amendments to the Constitution of the United States, all, or any of which Articles, when ratified by three fourths of the said Legislatures, to be valid to all intents and purposes, as part of the said Constitution; viz.

Articles in addition to, and Amendment of the Constitution of the United States of America, proposed by Congress, and ratified by the Legislatures of the several States, pursuant to the fifth Article of the original Constitution.

NOTE: The following text is a transcription of the first ten amendments to the Constitution in their original form. These amendments were ratified December 15, 1791, and form what is known as the "Bill of Rights."

AMENDMENT I

Congress shall make no law respecting an establishment of religion, or prohibiting the free exercise thereof; or abridging the freedom of speech, or of the press; or the right of the people peaceably to assemble, and to petition the Government for a redress of grievances.

AMENDMENT II

A well regulated Militia, being necessary to the security of a free State, the right of the people to keep and bear Arms, shall not be infringed.

AMENDMENT III

No Soldier shall, in time of peace be quartered in any house, without the consent of the Owner, nor in time of war, but in a manner to be prescribed by law.

AMENDMENT IV

The right of the people to be secure in their persons, houses, papers, and effects, against unreasonable searches and seizures, shall not be violated, and no Warrants shall issue, but upon probable cause, supported by Oath or affirmation, and particularly describing the place to be searched, and the persons or things to be seized.

AMENDMENT V

No person shall be held to answer for a capital, or otherwise infamous crime, unless on a presentment or indictment of a Grand Jury, except in cases arising in the land or naval forces, or in the Militia, when in actual service in time of War or public danger; nor shall any person be subject for the same offence to be twice put in jeopardy of life or limb; nor shall be compelled in any criminal case to be a witness against himself, nor be deprived of life, liberty, or property, without due process of law; nor shall private property be taken for public use, without just compensation.

AMENDMENT VI

In all criminal prosecutions, the accused shall enjoy the right to a speedy and public trial, by an impartial jury of the State and district wherein the crime shall have been committed, which district shall have been previously ascertained by law, and to be informed of the nature and cause of the accusation; to be confronted with the witnesses against him; to have compulsory process for obtaining witnesses in his favor, and to have the Assistance of Counsel for his defence.

AMENDMENT VII

In Suits at common law, where the value in controversy shall exceed twenty dollars, the right of trial by jury shall be preserved, and no fact tried by a jury, shall be otherwise re-examined in any Court of the United States, than according to the rules of the common law.

AMENDMENT VIII

Excessive bail shall not be required, nor excessive fines imposed, nor cruel and unusual punishments inflicted.

AMENDMENT IX

The enumeration in the Constitution, of certain rights, shall not be construed to deny or disparage others retained by the people.

AMENDMENT X

The powers not delegated to the United States by the Constitution, nor prohibited by it to the States, are reserved to the States respectively, or to the people.

APPENDIX C

THE GETTYSBURG ADDRESS

Four score and seven years ago our fathers brought forth on this continent, a new nation, conceived in Liberty, and dedicated to the proposition that all men are created equal.

Now we are engaged in a great civil war, testing whether that nation, or any nation so conceived and so dedicated, can long endure. We are met on a great battle-field of that war. We have come to dedicate a portion of that field, as a final resting place for those who here gave their lives that that nation might live. It is altogether fitting and proper that we should do this.

But, in a larger sense, we can not dedicate—we can not consecrate—we can not hallow—this ground. The brave men, living and dead, who struggled here, have consecrated it, far above our poor power to add or detract. The world will little note, nor long remember what we say here, but it can never forget what they did here. It is for us the living, rather, to be dedicated here to the unfinished work which they who fought here have thus far so nobly advanced. It is rather for us to be here dedicated to the great task remaining before us—that from these honored dead we take increased devotion to that cause for which they gave the last full measure of devotion—that we here highly resolve that these dead shall not have died in vain—that this nation, under God, shall have a new birth of freedom—and that government of the people, by the people, for the people, shall not perish from the earth.

—ABRAHAM LINCOLN, NOVEMBER 19, 1863

12 RULES FOR RADICALS

by SAUL ALINKSY

RULE 1: "POWER IS NOT ONLY WHAT YOU HAVE, BUT WHAT THE ENEMY THINKS YOU HAVE." Power is derived from 2 main sources—money and people. "Have-Nots" must build power from flesh and blood. (These are two things of which there is a plentiful supply. Government and corporations always have a difficult time appealing to people, and usually do so almost exclusively with economic arguments.)

RULE 2: "NEVER GO OUTSIDE THE EXPERTISE OF YOUR PEOPLE." It results in confusion, fear and retreat. Feeling secure adds to the backbone of anyone. (Organizations under attack wonder why radicals don't address the "real" issues. This is why. They avoid things with which they have no knowledge.)

RULE 3: "WHENEVER POSSIBLE, GO OUTSIDE THE EXPERTISE OF THE ENEMY." Look for ways to increase insecurity, anxiety and uncertainty. (This happens all the time. Watch how many organizations under attack are blind-sided by seemingly irrelevant arguments that they are then forced to address.)

RULE 4: "MAKE THE ENEMY LIVE UP TO ITS OWN BOOK OF RULES." If the rule is that every letter gets a reply, send 30,000 letters. You can kill them with this because no one can possibly obey all of their own rules. (This is a serious rule. The besieged entity's very credibility and reputation is at stake, because if activists catch it lying or not living up to its commitments, they can continue to chip away at the damage.)

RULE 5: "RIDICULE IS MAN'S MOST POTENT WEAPON." There is no defense. It's irrational. It's infuriating. It also works as a key pressure point to force the enemy into concessions. (Pretty crude, rude and mean, huh? They want to create anger and fear.)

RULE 6: "A GOOD TACTIC IS ONE YOUR PEOPLE ENJOY." They'll keep doing it without urging and come back to do more. They're doing their thing, and will even suggest better ones. (Radical activists, in this sense, are no different that any other human being. We all avoid "un-fun" activities, and but we revel at and enjoy the ones that work and bring results.)

RULE 7: "A TACTIC THAT DRAGS ON TOO LONG BECOMES A DRAG." Don't become old news. (Even radical activists get bored. So to keep them excited and involved, organizers are constantly coming up with new tactics.)

RULE 8: "KEEP THE PRESSURE ON. NEVER LET UP." Keep trying new things to keep the opposition off balance. As the opposition masters one approach, hit them from the flank with something new. (Attack, attack, attack from all sides, never giving the reeling organization a chance to rest, regroup, recover and re-strategize.)

RULE 9: "THE THREAT IS USUALLY MORE TERRIFYING THAN THE THING ITSELF." Imagination and ego can dream up many more consequences than any activist. (Perception is reality. Large organizations always prepare a worst-case scenario, something that may be furthest from the activists' minds. The upshot is that the organization will expend enormous time and energy, creating in its own collective mind the direst of conclusions. The possibilities can easily poison the mind and result in demoralization.)

RULE 10: "IF YOU PUSH A NEGATIVE HARD ENOUGH, IT WILL PUSH THROUGH AND BECOME A POSITIVE." Violence from the other side can win the public to your side because the public sympathizes with the underdog. (Unions used this tactic. Peaceful [albeit loud] demonstrations during the heyday of unions in the early to mid-20th Century incurred management's wrath, often in the form of violence that eventually brought public sympathy to their side.)

RULE 11: "THE PRICE OF A SUCCESSFUL ATTACK IS A CONSTRUCTIVE ALTERNATIVE." Never let the enemy score points because you're caught without a solution to the problem. (Old saw: If you're not part of the solution, you're part of the problem. Activist organizations have an agenda, and their strategy is to hold a place at the table, to be given a forum to wield their power. So, they have to have a compromise solution.)

RULE 12: "PICK THE TARGET, FREEZE IT, PERSONALIZE IT, AND POLARIZE IT." Cut off the support network and isolate the target from sympathy. Go after people and not institutions; people hurt faster than institutions. (This is cruel, but very effective. Direct, personalized criticism and ridicule works.)

APPENDIX E

THE POLITICS OF LYING

by BILL FEDERER

WND EXCLUSIVE: BILL FEDERER SEES OBAMA STRATEGY
CLEARLY IN MACHIAVELLI QUOTES — 11/12/2013

"If you like your health-care plan, you can keep it. Period." —President Barak Obama

Americans are stunned by the president's disregard for his promise.

This makes perfect sense, though, when one reads the popular political handbook written by Niccolo Machiavelli in 1515 titled "The Prince":

"The promise given was a necessity of the past: the word broken is a necessity of the present."

"A wise ruler ought never to keep faith when by doing so it would be against his interests."

"A prince never lacks legitimate reasons to break his promise."

Machiavelli explained how people are inclined to believe lies from their leaders:

"One who deceives will always find those who allow themselves to be deceived."

"Men are so simple and so much inclined to obey immediate needs that a deceiver will never lack victims for his deceptions."

"Men are so simple and yield so readily to the desires of the moment that he who will trick will always find another who will suffer to be tricked."

Machiavelli taught that "the end justifies the means." If a leader is convinced his "end" is good, any "means" necessary to achieve that end is permitted:

"Politics have no relation to morals."

"No enterprise is more likely to succeed than one concealed from the enemy until it is ripe for execution."

"It is double pleasure to deceive the deceiver."

Machiavelli promised "change":

"One change always leaves the way open for the establishment of others."

"Whosoever desires constant success must change his conduct with the times."

"I'm not interested in preserving the status quo; I want to over-throw it."

As Americans are awakening to the realization that a Machiavellian leader could actually lie to them, they may be curious to read how Machiavelli instructs a leader to treat his opponents:

"If an injury has to be done to a man it should be so severe that his vengeance need not be feared."

"Severities should be dealt out all at once, so that their suddenness may give less offense; benefits ought to be handed out drop by drop, so that they may be relished the more."

"The new ruler must determine all the injuries that he will need to inflict. He must inflict them once and for all."

Machiavelli continued:

"Men ought either to be indulged or utterly destroyed, for if you merely offend them they take vengeance, but if you injure them greatly they are unable to retaliate, so that the injury done to a man ought to be such that vengeance cannot be feared."

"Men should be either treated generously or destroyed, because they take revenge for slight injuries—for heavy ones they cannot."

"Whoever conquers a free town and does not demolish it commits a great error and may expect to be ruined himself."

Are people beginning to fear government? Machiavelli recommended a leader make that happen, too:

"Men shrink less from offending one who inspires love than one who inspires fear."

"Since it is difficult to join them together, it is safer to be feared than to be loved when one of the two must be lacking."

"It is better to be feared than loved, if you cannot be both."

"It is much more secure to be feared than to be loved."

NOTES

CHAPTER 1

1. Patrick Brennan, "Obama's Infanticide Votes," *National Review Online*, February 29, 2012, http://nationalreview.com/articles/292204/obama-s-infanticide-votes-patrick-brennan.
2. Josh Gerstein, "Eric Holder: Black Panther case focus demeans 'my people,'" *Under the Radar* (Politico blog), March 1, 2011, http://www.politico.com/blogs/joshgerstein/0311/Eric_Holder_Black_Panther_case_focus_demeans_my_people.html.
3. Jim Hoft, "Eric Holder: Black Panther Case Demeans 'My People,'" *Gateway Pundit* (blog), March 1, 2011, http://www.thegatewaypundit.com/2011/03/eric-holder-black-panther-case-demeans-my-people/; emphasis added.
4. See http://latimesblogs.latimes.com/showtracker/2009/11/modren-family-eric-stonestreet-reveals-camerons-clownfilled-past.html and http://flavorwire.com/newswire/modern-familys-eric-stonestreet-talks-gay-agenda-sort-of/, among others.
5. *Modern Family* Wiki, http://modernfamily.wikia.com/wiki/Mistery_Date.
6. Jeffrey Richman, "Mistery Date," *Modern Family*, season 4, episode 8, directed by Beth McCarthy-Miller, aired November 14, 2012. Transcript available from Hypnoweb.net, at http://modern-family.hypnoweb.net/episodes/saison-4/mistery-date/script-vo-408.192.1236/.
7. Greg Daniels et al., "The Target," *The Office*, season 9, episode 8, directed by Brent Forrester, aired November 29, 2012. Transcript available from Springfield! Springfield! At http://www.springfieldspringfield.co.uk/view_episode_scripts.php?tv-show=the-office-us&episode=s09e08.
8. "What is a Conservative?" YouTube video, 5:45, posted by MRCTV.org, November 11, 2013, https://www.youtube.com/watch?v=LjL3m9cmvgQ.
9. Todd Beamon and John Bachman, "Brinkley Book: Cronkite Had 'Liberal Bias,'" NewsMax, June 4, 2012, http://www.newsmax.com/US/brinkley-cronkite-liberal-bias/2012/06/04/id/441177.
10. See "Walter Cronkite and the New World Order," YouTube video, 8:07, posted by Toxic Shamrock, April 24, 2009, http://www.youtube.com/watch?v=OfgFvdSPF70.
11. Quotations from Karen Siegemund in this chapter are from an interview conducted by Ann-Marie Murrell on August 17, 2013, before the Rage Against the Media rally in Los Angeles, where Siegemund spoke. Siegemund's comments can be seen in Murrell's

article "Rage Against the Media Rally in Los Angeles," posted on the *PolitiChicks* blog on the same day, at http://politichicks.tv/column/rage-against-the-media-rally-in-los-angeles/#roWxaGhqPhigyjyz.99.

CHAPTER 3

1.   Gina Loudon, "Labels, lunatics and fringe," *WND Commentary*, February 9, 2014, http://www.wnd.com/2014/02/labels-lunatics-and-fringe/#0v8JJKSVUlfTM3sq.99.
2.   Gina Loudon and Dathan Paterno, *Ladies and Gentleman: Why the Survival of Our Republic Depends on the Revival of Honor* (Chattanooga: God and Country Press, 2012), 112.

CHAPTER 5

1.   Daniel Greenfield, "Hate Is the Force that Gives the Left Meaning," *Sultan Knish* (blog), February 6, 2014, http://sultanknish.blogspot.com/2014/02/hate-is-force-that-gives-left-meaning.html.
2.   "Tell Congress to Stop its Attacks on Planned Parenthood," official website of Stop the War on Women, paid for by EMILY'S List and MoveOn.org, accessed March 27, 2014, http://stopthewaronwomen.com/take-action/tell-congress-stop-its-attacks-planned-parenthood.
3.   "Sex-Selective Abortion Thrives in America, Courtesy Planned Parenthood," YouTube video, 7:25, posted by LiveActionFilms, May 29, 2012, http://liveaction.org/blog/sex-selective-abortion-thrives-in-america-courtesy-planned-parenthood/.
4.   Lila Rose, "Why are we still funding Planned Parenthood?" *Daily Caller*, Opinion, March 25, 2013, http://dailycaller.com/2013/03/25/why-are-we-still-funding-planned-parenthood/#ixzz2PRutyQGt.
5.   "Tell Congress to Stop its Attacks on Planned Parenthood."
6.   "On the Situation of Afghan Women," RAWA, http://www.rawa.org/wom-view.htm; accessed March 27, 2014.
7.   Pamela Gellar, "Voiceless march: Women against sharia march in Afghanistan," *Atlas Shrugs* (Pamela Gellar blog), July 11, 2012, http://pamelageller.com/2012/07/voiceless-march-women-against-sharia-march-in-afghanistan.html/.
8.   Owen Bowcott, "Afghanistan worst place in the world for women, but India in top five," *Guardian* (UK), June 14, 2011, http://www.theguardian.com/world/2011/jun/15/worst-place-women-afghanistan-india.
9.   Pamela Gellar, "Lara Logan's Vicious, Violent Gang-Rape, Media's Silence = Sanction," *Atlas Shrugs*, February 19, 2011, http://pamelageller.com/2011/02/lara-logans-vicious-violent-gang-rape-medias-silencesanction.html/
10. Mayy El Sheikh and David D. Kirkpatrick, "Rise in Sexual Assaults in Egypt Sets Off Clash over Blame," *New York Times*, Middle East, March 25, 2013, http://www.nytimes.com/2013/03/26/world/middleeast/egyptian-women-blamed-for-sexual-assaults.html?src=un&feedurl=http://json8.nytimes.com/pages/world/middleeast/index.jsonp&_r=3&.
11. "Day 1: Meet Hania Moheeb, Egypt," Nobel Women's Initiative, November 25, 2013, http://nobelwomensinitiative.org/2013/11/day-1-meet-hania-moheeb-egypt/.

12. Lydia Goodman, "Egypt: Hell on Earth," *PolitiChicks*, March 30, 2013, http://politichicks. tv/column/egypt-hell-on-earth/.

13. Katherine Weber, "Report: Forced Abortion in China Takes Life of 7-Month Boy," *Christian Post (CP Asia)*, March 25, 2013, http://global.christianpost.com/news/report-forced-abortion-in-china-takes-life-of-7-month-boy-92620/#e3Lll0dCorFof5Ft.99.

14. Bowcott, "Afghanistan worst place in the world for women."

15. Rob Crilly, "1,000 Pakistani women and girls honour killing victims," *Telegraph* (UK), March 22, 2012, http://www.telegraph.co.uk/news/worldnews/asia/pakistan/9160515/1000-Pakistani-women-and-girls-honour-killing-victims.html.

16. The quotes that follow are from Meghan Daum, "Carrie Prejean vs. Perez Hilton," *Los Angeles Times*, April 25, 2009, http://articles.latimes.com/2009/apr/25/opinion/oe-daum25.

17. Luchina Fisher, "Perez Hilton 'Floored' by Miss California," ABC News, April 20, 2009, http://abcnews.go.com/Entertainment/Television/story?id=7381893.

18. Drew Magary, "What the Duck," *GQ*, January 2014, http://www.gq.com/entertainment/television/201401/duck-dynasty-phil-robertson?currentPage=2.

19. Drew Magary, "The Devil and Phil Robertson: My Day with *Duck Dynasty*," *Deadspin*, December 18, 2013, http://deadspin.com/the-devil-and-phil-robertson-my-day-with-duck-dynasty-1485612609.

20. *Merriam-Webster Dictionary*, s.v. "intolerant," http://www.merriam-webster.com/dictionary/intolerant; accessed March 28, 2013.

21. Evan Sayet, "Why the Left Hates Sarah Palin," *FrontPageMag*, January 18, 2011, http://www.frontpagemag.com/2011/evan-sayet/why-the-left-hates-sarah-palin/2/.

22. Jeff Poor, "Low-brow: Bill Maher says Sarah Palin is a 'dumb twat,'" *FrontPageMag*, January 18, 2011, http://dailycaller.com/2011/03/19/low-brow-bill-maher-says-sarah-palin-is-a-dumb-twat/.

23. Jim Hoft, "Liberal Icon Bill Maher: Sarah Palin's Children Are 'Inbred Weirdos'," Gateway Pundit, July 18, 2011, http://www.thegatewaypundit.com/2011/07/liberal-icon-bill-maher-sarah-palins-children-are-inbred-weirdos-video/.

24. Noel Sheppard, "Despicable: MSNBC's Bashir Wishes Sarah Palin Would Be Defecated, Urinated On," *NewsBusters*, November 15, 2013, http://newsbusters.org/blogs/noel-sheppard/2013/11/15/despicable-msnbcs-bashir-wishes-sarah-palin-would-be-defecated-urinat.

25. "Sarah Palin Church," GodVoter.org, http://www.godvoter.org/Sarah-Palin-church.html.

26. Twitchy staff, "Actress Stacey Dash announces support for Romney; Disgruntled Dems attack; Update: Some defend, some hope she was hacked," *Twitchy*, October 7, 2012, http://twitchy.com/2012/10/07/actress-stacey-dash-announces-support-for-romney-disgruntled-dems-attack/.

27. "An Important Message from Eva Longoria Parker," YouTube video, 0:30, posted by TheEllenShow, November 12, 2010, http://www.youtube.com/watch?v=OB9S5T4e7Vo.

28. Twitchy staff, "Obama campaign co-chair Eva Longoria deletes retweet calling women and minorities 'stupid' for supporting Romney," *Twitchy*, October 17, 2012, http://twitchy.com/2012/10/17/obama-campaign-co-chair-eva-longoria-deletes-retweet-calling-women-and-minorities-stupid-for-supporting-romney/.

29. "Madonna on Bullying in Media," YouTube video, 4:44, posted by TheEllenShow, November 9, 2010, https://www.youtube.com/watch?v=pcLErJd6EtA&playnext=1&list=PLA1CBDAD D7A801A65&feature=results_video.

30. FoxNews.com, "Madonna calls Obama a 'black Muslim,' says she'll strip onstage if he wins new term," Fox 411, September 25, 2012, http://www.foxnews.com/ entertainment/2012/09/25/madonna-calls-president-obama-black-muslim-says-shell-strip-onstage-if-wins/#ixzz29f1DHQno.

31. Dickjonas, "Christina Aguilera and Cher Speak Out Against Bullies" *Starzlife*, December 13, 2010, http://www.starzlife.com/20101213/christina-aguilera-and-cher-speak-out-against-bullies/.

32. "Cher: Reason number 1436 why I hope Romney wins," *Hack Wilson* (blog), May 8, 2012, http://hackwilson.blogspot.com/2012/05/cher-reason-number-1436-why-i-hope.html.

33. Daniel Kurtzman, "Wanda Sykes' Limbaugh Joke Stirs Controversy," About.com, May 11, 2009, http://politicalhumor.about.com/b/2009/05/11/wanda-sykes-limbaugh-joke-stirs-controversy.htm.

34. David Folkenflik, "Totenberg on Helms Comment: 'It Was A Stupid Remark,'" *The Two-Way* (blog), October 26, 2010, http://www.npr.org/blogs/thetwo-way/2010/10/26/130838719/ totenberg-on-helms-remark-stupidest-thing-she-s-said-on-tv.

CHAPTER 6

1. Alejandro Gomez Monteverde, Patrick Million, and Leo Severino, *Bella*, directed by Alejandro Gomez Monteverde (Los Angeles: Roadside Attractions, 2006), film.

2. Brandon Cox, "Rick Warren on Muslims, Evangelism, and Missions" (transcript of an interview between Rick Warren, Cox, and the *Christian Post*), Pastors.com, p. 1, http:// pastors.com/rick-warren-on-muslims-evangelism-and-missions/, accessed March 28, 2014.

3. Xander Gibb, "When Will Your Political Evolution Begin???? 'Wake Up America & Smell the Lies,'" *Xandermonium* (blog), November 5, 2013, http://www.xandergibb.com/personal-political-evolution.htm#sthash.LbhXjU18.riiMJxh7.dpuf.

4. Jonathan Haidt, *The Righteous Mind: Why Good People Are Divided by Politics and Religion*, 1st Vintage ed. (New York: Pantheon, 2013).

5. Holman W. Jenkins Jr., "Jonathan Haidt: He Knows Why We Fight: Conservative or liberal, our moral instincts are shaped by evolution to strengthen 'us' against 'them,'" *Wall Street Journal*, June 29, 2012, http://online.wsj.com/news/articles/SB10001424052702303830204 577446512522582648.

6. Haidt, *The Righteous Mind*, 353, 354–55.

7. Jonathan Haidt, *The Righteous Mind* (Google eBook), unabridged ed. (New York: Random House, 2012).

CHAPTER 7

1. Andrew Breitbart, *Righteous Indignation: Excuse Me While I Save the World* (Google eBook) (n.p.: Hachette Digital, 2011), chap. 10, par. 1.

2. Curtis M. Wong, Gay Voices (*HuffPost* blog), November 16, 2011, http://www.huffingtonpost. com/2011/11/16/victoria-jackson-politichicks-web-show_n_1097796.html.

3. Matt Cherette, November 17, 2011, http://gawker.com/5860394/politichicks-is-a-conservative-version-of-the-view-from-hell.

4. Perez Hilton, "Victoria Jackson Releases Anti-Gay, Anti-Muslim Web TV Show," Perez Hilton's blog, November 17, 2011, http://perezhilton.com/2011-11-17-victoria-jackson-politichicks#sthash.38ddQcaH.dpuf.

5. Alex Alvarez, "TGIF: This Week, God Gave Us the *PolitiChicks*, Victoria Jackson's Online Answer to The View," *Mediaite* (blog), November 18, 2011, http://www.mediaite.com/online/tgif-this-week-god-gave-us-the-politichicks-victoria-jacksons-online-answer-to-the-view/.

6. By the way, I'm always looking for strong, conservative women writers. Although I am much more selective than I was in the beginning, if you would like to be considered a Nationwide PolitiChick writer, please send a sample of your writing to annmarie@politichicks.tv.

7. Ann-Marie Murrell, "Death of a Hero," *PolitiChicks* blog, March 1, 2013, http://politichicks.tv/column/death-of-a-hero/.

CHAPTER 8

1. Brian Schmidt, "Who's the Farthest of Them All? Scores Show State Legislator Leanings," *Missouri Wonk*, November 22, 2013, http://mowonk.com/2013/11/22/whos-the-farthest-of-them-all-scores-show-state-legislator-leanings/.

2. Richard Stengel, "One Document, Under Siege," *Time*, June 23, 2011, http://content.time.com/time/nation/article/0,8599,2079445,00.html, p. 5.

3. Thomas Sowell, "July 4th," *Townhall*, June 28, 2011, http://townhall.com/columnists/thomassowell/2011/06/28/july_4th/page/full.

4. Phyllis Schlafly, "Do Party Platforms Really Matter?" *The Phyllis Schlafly Report,* 41, no. 12 (July 2008), http://www.eagleforum.org/psr/2008/july08/psrjuly08.html.

5. John Woolley and Gerhard Peters, "Republican Party of 2000," Political Party Platforms: Parties Receiving Electoral Votes 1840–2012, The American Presidency Project, July 31, 2000, http://www.presidency.ucsb.edu/ws/?pid=25849.

6. Michael O'Brien, "Priebus: GOP platform 'not the platform of Mitt Romney'" NBC News, August 21, 2012, http://firstread.nbcnews.com/_news/2012/08/21/13395825-priebus-gop-platform-not-the-platform-of-mitt-romney?lite.

7. Quoted in Schlafly, "Do Party Platforms Really Matter?"

8. Hadley Freeman, "Christian Louboutin: How killer heels conquered fashion," *Guardian* (UK), March 19, 2010, http://www.theguardian.com/lifeandstyle/2010/mar/19/christian-louboutin-high-heels.

9. *Wikipedia*, s.v. "William F. Buckley, Jr." (section: "Buckley Rule"), http://en.wikipedia.org/wiki/William_F._Buckley, accessed March 31, 2014.

10. Thomas Schmitz, American Grizzlies chairman, quoted in an e-mail interview with Dr. Gina Loudon, January 2014.

11. David Foster Wallace, *Up, Simba!* (New York: Hachette Digital, 2000).

12. Isaiah Hankel, "15 Benefits of Being an Intelligent Misfit," *Experiments in Cheeky Science* (blog), accessed March 9, 2014, http://www.isaiahhankel.com/misfit?utm_content=bufferb8b14&utm_medium=social&utm_source=plus.google.com&utm_campaign=buffer.

13. Andy Hunt, *Pragmatic Thinking and Learning: Refactor Your Wetware* (n.p.: Pragmatic Bookshelf, 2008), 4.

CHAPTER 10

1. William F. Buckley Jr., "Our Mission Statement," *National Review Online*, November 19, 1955, http://www.nationalreview.com/articles/223549/our-mission-statement/william-f-buckley-jr.
2. The Cronkite quotations that follow are as quoted in "Walter Cronkite: Liberal Media Icon," Media Research Center, March 15, 2006, http://www.mrc.org/node/29184.
3. "Cronkite, Satan, and Hillary Oh My!" YouTube video, 3:50, posted by SilverShieldGrp, uploaded on August 18, 2009, http://www.youtube.com/watch?v=SpOJgmHK9ls.

CHAPTER 12

1. Josh Goldsmith, Cathy Yuspa, and Diane Drake, *What Women Want*, directed by Nancy Meyers (Icon Entertainment, 2000), film.
2. Kitty Werthmann's comments in this chapter are from a speech she gave, but she also wrote her story in an article posted on the website of Saint Marguerite Bourgeoys Roman Catholic Church, at http://www.stmarguerite.org/political.html, accessed April 1, 2014.
3. Theodore Roosevelt, from his speech "Citizenship in a Republic" delivered at the Sorbonne, in Paris, France, on April, 23, 1910.

INDEX

A

ABC, 18, 23, 34, 74, 87–88, 94, 95, 97, 153. *See also Modern Family*; *Wife Swap*

abortion, 11, 40, 47, 62, 66–67, 69, 70, 118, 126, 142, 145, 147, 158, 170

ACLU, 150

actions that will make a difference, 116–20

activitists (grassroots), four things they must do, 127

adoption, story of Gina and John, 81–85

alcoholism, appear in film, 54

Afghanistan, plight of women in, 67

Afifi, Adel Abdel Maqsoud, 68

Alinsky, Saul, 119, 124

12 Rules for Radicals, 204–6

Al Jazeera, 88, 111

All in the Family, 61

amendments to the constitution. *See* Bill of Rights; Second Amendment

American Mother, the, 167

Angle, Sharron, 156

Angry Young Man theme, introduction into film, 59

anti-bullying campaigns, 78–79

antiestablishment movement takeover of Hollywood, 57

antihero, (in entertainment), 54, 57

antiwar, 5, 30, 57, 58, 158

Apartment, The (1960), 54

Arguing for the Constitution (Maikoski), 41

atheists in the battle against the church, 118

Atlas Shrugged (Rand), 11

Avalon, Frankie, 55

B

Bachmann, Michele, 109

backscatter X-ray, 16

Bajpai, Divya, 70

Ball, Lucille, 52, 59–60

Bashir, Martin, 76

Beame, "Abe," 32, 34

beauty pageant, 70–74

Beck, Glenn, 11, 26, 97

Behar, Joy (X. Gibb, on), 95

Benghazi scandal, 18, 25

Beyoncé, 167

Biden, Joe, 25

Bill of Rights, xviii, 41, 178, 188, 198–201

birth control, 46, 67, 69, 70, 130, 131, 170

Bledsoe, Jerry, 9, 13, 15, 17

blogging to make a difference, 117

Bonnie and Clyde, 57

Boone, Pat, 55

Bosley, Tom, 60

Bosstick, Jordan, 130

boundary crossing in 1960s entertainment, 57

Bow, Clara, 139

Brady Bunch, The, 17, 61

Brando, Marlon, 54

INDEX

Breitbart (news syndicate), 109, 110

Breitbart, Andrew, xii, xv, 105, 109, 112–14, 182

Brewer, Jan, 169

Brewer, Rosalind, 166

Brinkley, David, 24

British programming, conservative values in, 141

Brittany, Morgan, 109, 110, 112

chapters by, 27–37, 51–64, 137–47, 165–74

Brokaw, Tom, 157

Brown, Beckie, 111

Brown, Gene, 25–26, 114–15

Brown, Lisa, 4, 9, 13

Brown, Lou Ellen, 8, 11, 13, 25–26, 115

Buckley, William F., 129, 149

Bull, Bartle, 12

bully, the real (mainstream media), 146

Burns, Ursula, 166

Bush, George H. W., 6, 125

Bush, George W., 8, 9, 25, 129

C

candidate criteria for running for office, 156–57

Carter, Billy, 4–5

Carter, Jimmy, 4–5, 6, 33, 34

CBS, 22, 51, 61, 68, 153

celebrity war against conservatives, 76–80

Cher, 79

Chick-fil-A, 146, 155

child marriage, 70

China, plight of women in, 69

churchgoers, percentage who vote in a general election, 133

Churchill, Winston, 125

Clinton, Bill, 5–8, 62

Clinton, Hillary, 6, 10, 121, 154, 159, 169, 170

CNN, 16

Common Core, 111, 167, 172

conservatives

celebrity war against, 76–80

philosophical divide between liberals and (as explained by J. Haidt), 99–100

and "progressives," college students' impression of the difference between, 23

Constitution (US). *See* United States Constitution

"constitutional centrist" defined, 42

Cosby Show, The, 61

Covan, Willie, 31

CPAC (Conservative Political Action Conference), 109, 111, 114

criteria for people who should run for office (Murrell), 156–57

Cronkite, Walter, 7, 23–24, 29, 157–60

Cross, Jim, 14

crosses, removal of, 16, 150

Crouching Tiger, Hidden Dragon, 140

Cruz, Ted, 128

D

Daily Show with Jon Stewart, 23, 88, 108

Dallas (TV series), 34, 35, 140

Dash, Stacey, 77

David, Ari, 23

Day, Doris, 52, 56

Dean, James, 54

Declaration of Independence (text), 192–97

Dee, Sandra, 55

DeGeneres, Ellen, 167

Democratic Republic of the Congo (DRC), plight of women in, 67–68

Delta County, U.S.A., 34

Democratic Party, 7, 76, 117, 156

Desperate Housewives' actress's anti-bullying campaign, 77

DINOs (Democrats in Name Only), 117

Disney, 56–57, 59

Dole, Bob, 125, 126, 129

Donnelly, Tim, 155

Downton Abbey, 141

Down syndrome

percentage of children aborted, 82

story of Gina and John's adoption of a child with, 81–85

Dr. Phil, 22–23

drug use (in film), 57

Duck Dynasty's Phil Robertson, 74–75

E

Eagle Forum, 124
East of Eden (1955), 55
Easy Rider, 58
educating our children about the greatness of
    America, 172
Egypt, plight of women in, 68–69
Elder, Larry, 106, 161
elections, working on, 119
Engelbrecht, Catherine, 119
Erdoes, Mary Calahan, 166
establishment Republicans, 98
extramarital affairs, appearance in film, 54

F

Facebook, xviii, 11, 14–15, 91, 106, 111, 117,
    166
Face the Nation, 129, 132
Fallin, Mary, 169
family crisis, appearance in film, 54
Federer, Bill, "The Politics of Lying," 207–9
feminist movement, 58
Fonda, Henry, 60
forced marriage, 67, 70
Ford, Gerald, 33
foreign countries, booming and profitable
    entertainment industry of, 140
Forrest Gump (film), 173
Foster, David, 131–32
four things grassroots activists must do, 127
Fox Business, 182
Fox News, 12, 23, 48, 150, 151, 166, 182
France, Macey, 111
free speech, 42
freedom of speech, 199
Funicello, Annette, 55

G

Gaffney, Frank, 109
Gawker, 108
Gellar, Pamela, 67
general election, percentage of churchgoers who
    vote in a, 133

Gettysburg Address, 202–3
Gibb, Xander, 95–97
Gibson, Mel, 62
Gibson Girl, 139
Gill, Jack (husband of Morgan), 142–43
Gina's dad, 39–40, 43–48
Gina's mom, 43, 44, 45, 83, 84
Glory (film), 173
Goodman, Lydia, 69
GOP (Grand Old Party: the Republican Party),
    9, 66, 67, 68, 80, 100, 116, 149, 150, 151,
    153–54, 188. *See also* Republican Party
    what's wrong with the, 122–23
Gore, Al, 7, 9
GQ interview with Phil Robertson, 74
Graduate, The, 57
Graham, Jesse, 99
grandmothers, 167
Grandy, Fred, 109
grass roots, 100, 123–25
grassroots activists, four things they must do,
    127
Greenfield, Daniel, 65
Greenwood, Lee, 37
Grisham, John, 140
groupthink, 134
gun registration and confiscation by the Nazis,
    180
Gunsmoke, 53, 55

H

Haidt, Jonathan, 98–101
Haley, Nikki, 169
Hankel, Isaiah, 134
Hannity, Sean, xii, 37, 97
Harvey, Paul, 47
Hasselbeck, Elisabeth (X. Gibb, on), 95
haters, how to combat the slings and arrows
    of, 112–16
Helms, Jesse, 79
herd mentality, 134
Hilton, Perez, 72–74, 108
Hitler, Adolf, 179
Holder, Eric, 12–14

INDEX

Hollywood
  how to win back, 137–48
  in the '50s and '60s, 51–54
  in the '60s and '70s, 54–60
  in the '70s and beyond, 60–64
  and the transformation of our culture, 51–64
homosexuality, 74, 75
  in film, 58, 61
honor killings, 67, 70
House Resolution 416,
Hudson, Rock, 52, 56
Huffington Post, 108
Hunt, Andy, 135
Huntley, Chet, 24

I

interracial relationships, introduction in film, 58
intolerant, defined, 75
IRS, 18, 98, 119, 130, 132
Islamists in the battle against the church, 118

J

Jackson, Victoria, 107–9
Jennings, Peter, 7
Jihad Watch, 111
Johnson, Sonnie, 109, 110
Johnson, Van, 59
Jolie, Angelina, 167
Jones, Jenny, 107
Joseph, Dan, 23
"Julia" (from "The Life of Julia" Obama campaign piece), 170

K

Kennedy, John F., 6, 29, 31–32, 56–57
Kennedy, Robert, 31–32
King, Jr., Martin Luther, 58
Koch, Ed, 34
Kuhn, Maggie, 136

L

Ladies and Gentlemen (Loudon and Paterno), 43
Left, the: why they hate Sarah Palin (as observed by E. Sayet), 76
left and *right*, origin of the terms, 41
Legion of Decency, 54
letter-writing to make a difference, 117
Levin, Mark, 11–12
Lewinsky, Monica, 6, 62
liberalism
  the sacred morality of, 99
  Walter Cronkite on, 158
liberals, philosophical divide between conservatives and (as explained by J. Haidt), 99–100
Liberty Alliance, 105, 106, 107–10, 111
Liberty and Tyranny (Levin), 11, 12, 105
Limbaugh, Rush, 79, 97, 150, 161, 176
Lincoln, Abraham, Gettysburg Address, 202–3
Lincoln (film), 173
Live Action.org, 66
Livingston, Jo Anne, 109
Livingston, Luke, 109
Logan, Lara, 68
Lolita (1962 film), 59
Longoria, Eva, 78
Lost Weekend, The (1945), 54
Loudon, Gina, 22–23, 109, 110, 112, 171
  chapters by, 39–48, 81–102, 121–36, 175–90
Loudon, John, 45–46, 47, 81–87, 93, 94, 123, 133, 176, 177–78, 180, 181, 186, 187

M

Machiavelli, Niccolò, Obama strategy seen in quotes from, 207–9
Madonna, 78–79
Magary, Drew, 74–75
Maher, Bill, 76
Maikoski, Steven, 41
mainstream media (MSM), 7, 8, 17–18, 22, 24–25, 112, 113, 146
make a difference, what you can do to, 116–20
Malkin, Michelle, 78
Malone, Chris, 152

Mamet, David, 37
Mansfield, Jayne, 55
Marshall, Nick, 175
Martinez, Susana, 169
Matrix (film), 183–84
Mayer, Louis B., 52, 53
Mayer, Marissa, 166
McCain, John, 121, 129, 132
media, 7–9, 13, 17–18, 22–26, 58, 60, 86, 95, 112–13, 114, 128, 130, 139, 145–47, 149, 165, 170, 173. *See also* social media
Mediaite, 108
Media Research Center, 23, 158
men, the type conservative women want, 130–31
MGM, 31, 52, 53, 139
Mill, John Stuart, 133
Missouri Wonk, 123
models, young people's idealization of, 139
Modern Family, 18–19, 20–22, 26
Moheeb, Hania, 68
Monroe, Marilyn, 54, 139
moral matrix of American liberals, 99
Mother, the American, 167
Mother Teresa. *See* Teresa of Calcutta
Motion Picture Association of America, 59
motion pictures in the 1950s and '60s, 51–52
MoveOn.org, 65
moviegoing population in the 1960s, age of highest percentage of, 57
Mr. Selfridge (film), 141
Mr. Smith Goes to Washington (film), 173
MSM. *See* mainstream media
MSNBC, 16, 76, 126
Murrell, Ann-Marie, 108, 171, 189, 210n11
   chapters by, 3–26, 65–80, 105–20, 149–64
   introduction by, xvii–xix
Murrell, Mark, 5–6, 22, 77, 155
musicals, 52, 56, 139
musicians, young people's idealization of, 139
Muslim Brotherhood, 68

N

Nader, Ralph, 8
Nativity scenes, 16, 123
NBC, 18, 153
New Black Panther Party voter intimidation, 12
Newman, Paul, 54
Newsweek, 153
New World Order, 24, 158
New York Times, 153
9/11 (September 11, 2001, terrorist attacks), 4, 8–9, 56, 105, 159, 175, 177–78, 183,
1950s and '60s, cultural shift in entertainment in the, 51–54
1960s and '70s, cultural shift in entertainment in the, 54–60
1970s and beyond, cultural shift in entertainment in the, 60–64
1990s, decline of culture in the, 62–63
Nixon, Richard, 4, 6, 29, 33
Nosek, Brian, 99
NSA, 98, 130, 132
nudity (in film), 57, 59

O

Obama, Barack, 10, 11, 13, 16, 25, 26, 65, 66, 68, 79, 87, 121, 154, 157, 162–63, 207
Obamacare, 25, 132
Office, The (TV series), 18, 19–20, 21, 22
office, criteria for people who should for political, 156–57
O'Keefe, James, 119
"one child per family" rule in China, 69
Oswald, Lee Harvey, 29, 58

P – Q

Pakistan, plight of women in, 69–70
Palin, Sarah, 25, 76–77, 110, 129, 170, 171–72
   "Why the Left Hates Sarah Palin" (Sayet), 76
partial birth abortion, 11, 126
party platform, the case for a, 123–27

Passion of the Christ (film), 61

Patch of Blue, A (film), 58

Patriot, The (film), 173

Patriot Update, 15, 106, 107

Paul, Ron, 129

person, the power of a (the case for a party platform), 123–27

Pew Research, 133

Peyton Place (TV series), 34, 54

phone calling to make a difference, 117

Planned Parenthood, 40, 66, 68, 69, 82, 130

political correctness, 42, 147, 170

political office, criteria for people who run for, 156–57

PolitiChicks, 4, 15, 22, 69, 107–12, 114, 170
    how to become a writer for, 214n6 (chap. 7)

Power, Tyrone, Sr., 54

power
    of the pen (the press), 86, 181
    of a person (the case for a party platform), 123–27

Prager, Dennis, 111

prayer, removal from schools, 150

Preamble (to the Bill of Rights), 198

Prejean, Carrie, 72–75

Priebus, Reince, 126

progressives, 23, 42, 65, 67, 68, 69, 70, 76, 77, 150
    and "conservatives," college students' definition of the difference between, 23

pro-life, 40, 47, 82 107, 125

Project Veritas, 119

Proposition 14, 31

Puller, Lewis, Burwell "Chesty," 174

Putnam, George, 35

Rebel Without a Cause, 54

Red White Blue News, 14, 15, 105

Reid, Harry, 156

Republican National Coalition for Life, 125

Republican National Convention (*also* RNC), 116, 125

Republican Party, 100, 121, 122, 126, 127, 128, 150, 151, 153. *See also* GOP
    platform, 125–26

Republican "war on women," 65–66, 80

research of candidates, 154

Revolutionary Association of the Women of Afghanistan (RAWA), 67

Richards, Cecile, 66

Ride Along, 141–42

Righteous Mind, The (Haidt), 98–100

right wing, origin of the term, 41

RINOs (Republicans in Name Only), 125

RNC (Republican National Convention), 116, 125

Robertson, Phil, 74–75

rock and roll, 55, 58

Rometty, Virginia, 166

Romney, Mitt, 77, 78, 79, 126, 129, 154, 155

Roosevelt, Eleanor, 89

Roosevelt, Theodore, 181

Rose, Lila, 66

Ros-Lehtinen, Ilena, 69

Rove, Karl, 121, 126

Rubin, Jerry, 5

Ruby, Jack, 29, 58

rules for radicals (Alinsky's), 204–6

run for office, criteria for people who should, 156–67

R

Rachel, AlfonZo, 106, 109

Rage Against the Media, 25, 210n11

rape, 61, 63, 66, 67–68
    capital of the world, 67

Rather, Dan, 7, 157

Reagan, Michael, 15

Reagan, Ronald, 6, 7, 35, 36, 45, 127, 173

S

same-sex marriage, Carrie Prejean's response concerning, 73

Sandberg, Sheryl, 166

Santorum, Rick, 129

Saving Private Ryan, 173

Sayet, Evan, 76

Schiavo, Terry, 84

Schieffer, Bob, 128, 132
Schlafly, Phyllis, 124, 125
Schmidt, Sonya, 107
SEC, 98, 130, 132
Second Amendment, 112, 117, 199
September 11, 2001, terrorist attacks (aka 9/11),
    4, 8–9, 56, 105, 159, 175, 177–78, 183,
    184
sexual boundaries, crossing of (in 1960s film),
    57
Sherlock, 141
Siegemund, Karen, 25, 210n11
"silent majority," 21, 114, 116, 119, 149, 150
Simpson, O. J., 62
Sinise, Gary, xii, 37
social media, 23, 91, 96, 111, 114, 119, 147,
    165, 171
Soros, George, 24, 65
Sowell, Thomas, 124
special-needs child, Gina and John's adoption
    of a, 81–85
Spencer, Robert, 111
sports figures, young people's idealization of,
    139
stars, idealization of, 138–39
"statist," defined, 42
Stearns, Cliff, 66
Steele, Danielle, 140
Stewart, Jannique, 107, 108
Stewart, Jon, 23, 88
stoning of women, 70
Stop the War on Women (website), 65, 66
"swarm think," 134
Sykes, Wanda, 79

T

taboo subjects, insertion into entertainment,
    57, 59, 61
Taliban, 67
talking
    to friends and family about religion and
        politics, 117–18
    to your pastor about politics, 118
talk radio, 23, 150, 153

Taylor, Elizabeth, 139
Taylor, Robert, 54
T.E.A., origin of the term, 40
Tea Party, 25, 40, 150–51, 153, 171
Teen Mom, 63
telephoning to make a difference, 117
Temple, Shirley, 54
Ten Commandments, 64, 126, 150
Teresa of Calcutta, 135
Thatcher, Margaret, 27, 135
theocracy (as described by G. Loudon in *WND
    Commentary*), 41–42
Time magazine, 124
Top Gun (film), 173
Totenberg, Nina, 79
True the Vote, 119
TSA, 98, 131, 132
12 Rules for Radicals, Saul Alinksy's, 204–6
Twitter, xviii, 78, 106, 111, 117

U

United Nations, Cronkite on the United States'
    need to give up some sovereignty to the,
    158–59
United 93 (film), 173
United States Constitution, xviii, xix, 41, 42,
    89, 124, 126, 127, 150, 188, 189, 194,
    198–201

V

Vallorani, Brandon, 107
values, desire for, in entertainment in the '70s,
    61
van Susteren, Greta, 166
Vietnam War, 7, 30, 58
View, The, 95, 107, 108
violence in film, 57, 59, 63, 139
voter fraud, 119

INDEX

W–X

War in Afghanistan, 67
Warner, Jack, 52
Warner Bros., 36, 52, 53
Warren, Rick, 94
Warrior, Padmasree, 166
war on women
    real, in foreign countries, 67–70
    so-called, 65–66, 80, 170
Watts Riots, 30–31
Wayne, John, 52, 171
Webster, (senator), 84–85
welfare, 43, 131, 179
Werthmann, Kitty, 178–80, 182–83, 184,
    215n2 (chap. 12)
what you can do to make a difference, 116–20
Whitman, Meg, 166
Whittle, Bill, 109
Wife Swap, 23, 87–95, 97
Winfrey, Oprah, 22, 167
WND Exclusive: "The Politics of Lying"
    (Federer), 207–9
women
    advances of, 166–67
    churchgoing, percentage who vote in general
        elections, 133
    plight of
    in Afghanistan, 67
    in China, 69
    in the Democratic Republic of the Congo
        (DRC), 67–68
    in Egypt, 68–69
    in Pakistan, 69–70
    in politics, 169–70
    what real women want, 127–30
    what women *really* want, 130–31
    what women really *don't* want, 131–32
    so-called war on, 65–66, 80, 170
Woodward, Bob, 128, 132
Wordpress.com, 117
World War II, 52, 58
writing letters to make a difference, 117

Y

Yellen, Janet, 166
Yours, Mine and Ours (film), 59–60
youth
    shift from family entertainment to films
        catered to the, 57
    of today and misguided youth of yesterday,
        common denominator between the, 23

Z

Zaslow, Beverly, 109, 111

No publisher in the world has a higher percentage of *New York Times* bestsellers.

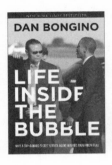

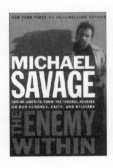

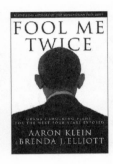

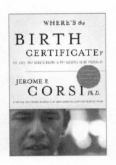

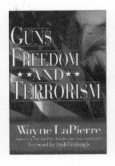

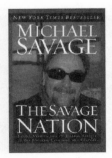